Marking Time

More Praise for Marking Time

"For Barbara Lundblad, the sermon is the meeting place where the Scripture text not only 'marks our time,' but where 'our experiences in this time of history also mark the text' in ways that are different from any interpretation in the past. What she provides in this marvelous book—a revision of her Lyman Beecher lectures at Yale Divinity School—is creative and insightful modeling for how the preacher can attend with equal seriousness to both biblical text and contemporary context, creating something altogether new in the preaching moment. With a scholar's careful attention to exegetical detail, a concerned citizen's well-read analysis of national and global issues, a pastor's love for the church and its people, and a poet's facility with language, Lundblad takes us deep into three biblical encounters—Elisha and the Shunammite woman, Jesus and the rich young ruler, and Philip and the Ethiopian eunuch—and invites us to mark our own time as we are also marked anew by these ever-revealing texts. As a bonus she also provides us with five of her marvelous sermons that carry her modeling all the way into the pulpit. I'm already counting the ways in which I can use this book in own my teaching of preaching. It is a gem!"

—Nora Tubbs Tisdale,
Clement-Muehl Professor of Homiletics,
Yale Divinity School

"Profound, practical, rooted in Biblical scholarship and relevant to our time, *Marking Time* is a gift to preachers and the congregations we serve. Lundblad addresses important questions (e.g., 'How do we preach a text we don't want to be in?') and demonstrates how 'God's living word speaks to us across centuries.' Read it, savor it, and encourage your congregation to do the same."

—Talitha Arnold, Senior Minister,
The United Church of Santa Fe,
A United Church of Christ

Marking Time

Preaching Biblical Stories in Present Tense

Barbara K. Lundblad

Abingdon Press
Nashville

MARKING TIME: PREACHING BIBLICAL STORIES IN PRESENT TENSE

Library of Congress Cataloging-in-Publication Data

Lundblad, Barbara K., 1944-
    Marking time : preaching biblical stories in present tense / Barbara K. Lundblad.
    p. cm.
    Includes bibliographical references.
    ISBN 978-0-687-04620-1 (pbk. : alk. paper)
    1. Preaching. 2. Storytelling—Religious aspects—Christianity. I. Title.

BV4222.L86 2007
251—dc22

2006038886

07 08 09 10 11 12 13 14 15 16—10 9 8 7 6 5 4 3 2 1

MANUFACTURED IN THE UNITED STATES OF AMERICA

To Robert Seaver, Mentor and Friend

For fifty-three years of helping students find their voices

and for bringing scripture texts to life whenever he reads

Contents

Preface ix

Acknowledgments xv

1. Marking Time: Reading Scripture at the River's Edge 1

2. It Will Be All Right: New Rubrics for the Holy Man's
   Room 19

3. The Camel and the Cash Machine: A Story We Try
   to Forget 33

4. Water on a Desert Road: Splashing in the Scroll of
   Isaiah 49

5. Standing Once More at the River's Edge 65

6. Sermons Preached at the River's Edge 79

   "Fragments" (After 9/11) 79

   "In God We Trust" (Revelation 18) 83

   "Turning Letters into Laws" (1 Corinthians 7) 88

   "What the Mighty Might Learn" (2 Kings 5) 94

   "No Prayer for Nineveh" (Jonah 2) 99

Notes 105

Preface

When I was a first year seminarian at Yale Divinity School, Frederick Buechner came to Marquand Chapel to give the Beecher Lectures. I hate to admit that I had never heard of him at the time, though I have read and borrowed his words regularly since then. He began by taking us back to the very beginning of the lecture series, more than one hundred years before that day in the chapel: On January 31, 1872, Henry Ward Beecher traveled to Yale to deliver the first of the Beecher Lectures on preaching, which had been established in memory of his father. Beecher's biographer writes:

> He had a bad night, not feeling well. Went to his hotel, got his dinner, lay down to take a nap. About two o'clock he got up and began to shave without having been able to get any plan of the lecture to be delivered within the hour. Just as he had his face lathered and was beginning to strop his razor, the whole thing came out of the clouds and dawned on him. He dropped his razor, seized his pencil, and dashed off the memoranda for it and afterwards cut himself badly, he said, thinking it out.[1]

Buechner went on to recall other lecturers who came after Henry Ward Beecher: Phillips Brooks, Dean Inge, Harry Emerson

Fosdick, and Reinhold Niebuhr. Then he focused his attention—and ours—on Pilate preparing to question Jesus:

> He pushes back from the desk and crosses his legs . . . Cigarette smoke drifts over the surface of the desk—the picture of his wife when she still had her looks, the onyx box from Caesar, the clay plaque with the imprint of his first son's hand on it, made while he was still a child in nursery school. Pilate squints at the man through the smoke and asks his question.[2]

No one stirred or coughed. I looked down from the balcony at the tops of people's heads, watching as some turned to those next to them, as though to say, "Did you hear that?" Others were bent down taking notes. Some of us in the balcony weren't quite ready to claim our place on the main floor. We hadn't preached much and we didn't know how much liberty we could take with the Bible. Would we dare to say Pilate was smoking a cigarette? Was there any textual evidence that he had received an onyx box from Caesar? We had spent the first semester learning to do something called *exegesis,* a word most of us had never heard before arriving on campus. Exegesis didn't encourage such imaginative speculation.

As he went on, it became clear this man named Buechner knew something about the life of the preacher. Perhaps he, too, had cut himself while shaving. He spoke in present tense, whether about Pilate or about preachers like the ones sitting there in front of him:

> So the sermon hymn comes to a close with a somewhat unsteady amen, and the organist gestures the choir to sit down. Fresh from breakfast with his wife and children and a quick runthrough of the Sunday papers, the preacher climbs the steps to the pulpit with his sermon in his hand. He hikes his black robe up at the knees so he will not trip over it on the way up. His mouth is a little dry. He has cut himself shaving . . .[3]

But we hadn't—cut ourselves shaving, I mean. That was the problem—all that shaving and the list of male lecturers and

Pontius Pilate and the preacher who had breakfast with his wife. The year was 1977. There were senior women who had begun their studies when the seminary was overwhelmingly male. When I arrived at school in the fall of 1976, I discovered a very robust Women's Center directed by women who were unapologetically feminist. I had barely discovered feminism before I headed east from Minnesota, but I soon found myself making up for lost time. Frederick Buechner walked into this lively feminist community without warning. After his first lecture, some women confronted him about all that shaving, all those male images, and all those men. He agreed to meet with women students that very afternoon.

The Women's Center was a lovely space on the ground floor of Bacon House, next door to where I lived. A stunning mural of strong women covered one entire wall. Gigantic homemade pillows were the only furniture in the room. Frederick Buechner sat there, cross-legged on a giant pillow, surrounded by women who were not shy in sharing their perspectives on his lecture.

"All of your images were male."

"You gave no hint that women were preachers, only preachers' wives!"

"Pilate got too much attention and you made him so very male—all that smoking and the picture of his wife. Was it necessary to say she used to be better looking?"

He was very gracious and seemed utterly perplexed, as though he had come from a far country and didn't know the language. He did not protest nor become defensive, nor did he revise his remaining lectures in any way discernible to us. Looking back now over thirty years, I am grateful for his generosity in sitting with us and listening so attentively. I am equally grateful for the women who dared to raise questions that hadn't yet occurred to me as we sat together on those giant pillows. Frederick Buechner spoke from his own experience and from the deep well of his own creativity, drawing us into the heart of the gospel and into our own lives in ways we couldn't have predicted. At a later time, we might have encouraged him to acknowledge his "social location" as feminists have urged male theologians to do—and as womanists have challenged white feminists to do. Now I realize that his power and presence as a writer and preacher came from the truth inside his own particular skin. He could not have spoken as we insisted. Yet most of us sitting in the balcony in 1977 have not forgotten what he said. The published version of his lectures, *Telling the Truth: The Gospel as Tragedy, Comedy & Fairy Tale*, sits on my bookshelf between Brueggemann and Buttrick, the pages dog-eared from regular visits. Some of us probably missed the full wonder of Buechner's lectures because our own experiences got in the way. He missed some of us because his own particularity both deepened and limited his pictures. Thinking back to that day in the chapel and that afternoon in the Women's Center has reminded me that we bring who we are into the *listening* as well as the *speaking*.

"The preacher pulls the little cord that turns on the lectern light," Buechner said, "and deals out his note cards like a river-boat gambler."[4] I suppose we thought that description was far too male at the time, yet we stayed to hear the rest of what he had to say. Up there in the balcony, we put aside much of what got in the way and listened in spite of ourselves. We were there at the end to hear what the man at the lectern said just before he turned off the light:

> Let the preacher tell the truth . . . which is that it is into the depths of his absence that God makes himself present in such unlikely ways and to such unlikely people that old Sarah and Abraham and maybe when the time comes even Pilate and Job and Lear and Henry Ward Beecher and you and I laugh till the tears run down our cheeks.[5]

By the time I stood at the chapel lectern to give the Beecher Lectures in 2000, three women had joined the 127-year-old procession before me. I am certain that my own particularity shaped my engagement with the biblical texts and the lectures that emerged from those encounters. There were probably some sitting in Marquand Chapel who couldn't hear what I said or who heard what I said and experienced dissonance with their own lives.

In many ways, my lectures were more like long sermons—an occupational hazard of being in the parish longer than in the academy. Since each lecture began with a biblical text, I asked my colleague Robert Seaver if he would come to read scripture for one of the lectures. Bob taught at Union Theological Seminary for fifty-three years before retiring for a second time in 2005. He not only came the first day but made the trip from New York to New Haven for all three lectures. There is no way to describe on paper what his reading is like: not loud or churchy, not dramatic or theatrical. He doesn't draw out the word *Gawd* as though the word had no connection with this earth. I do know such reading doesn't happen without long preparation. Bob reads and rereads the text in several different versions; he talks to himself and walks around the room until the words get deep inside him. When he reads a text—even the most familiar text—I feel as though I have heard it for the very first time.

On the morning the lectures began, I was alone in Marquand Chapel, checking the height of the lectern and getting the feel of the space from that vantage point. Mostly, I was trying to ward off anxiety—even though I had started writing much farther in advance than Henry Ward Beecher did while shaving that long-ago afternoon. Bob arrived early and came into the chapel while I was standing at the lectern. He told me to stay right where I was and do some of the exercises he used in his voice building classes. We had taught together so I knew what was coming. *Say your first few sentences in a straight line like a monotone chant. Then go up a half step and do the same thing. Now speak the same lines again and let your voice swoop way up at the end of each line. Don't just stand there—raise your arm up as you swoop.* I looked through the windows in the chapel door to see if anybody was lurking outside. Seeing no one, I did exactly what he asked me to do, chanting and swooping my way through the tension. Of course, that was exactly what Bob had in mind.

An hour later, I listened as he read the very long text from 2 Kings, chapter 4. When I pulled the little cord to turn on the light, I had heard the story as though for the first time, and that made all the difference. I dedicate this book to Robert Seaver in gratitude for fifty-three years of helping students find their voices and for ten years of life-giving friendship.

Barbara Lundblad
Epiphany 2007

Acknowledgments

This book has been coauthored by a wide circle of colleagues, friends, and family. First of all, I am deeply grateful to the faculty of Yale Divinity School and former dean Richard Wood for inviting me to give the Lyman Beecher Lectures in the fall of 2000. As I looked out into the chapel I was encouraged to see people who had been my teachers and my classmates looking back at me. I also give thanks to Union Theological Seminary for a sabbatical semester that coincided with preparation for the lectures. At the risk of forgetting some who have helped along the way, I give thanks in particular ways to the names that follow:

. . . to Rabbi Margaret Moers Wenig for reminding me of the story of the Shunammite woman and for sharing insights about that text from the Jewish tradition. I will always be grateful for the time we shared worshiping in the same building while I was the pastor of Our Saviour's Atonement Lutheran Church and she the rabbi of Beth Am;

. . . to Edwina (Wyn) Wright, Director of Languages at Union, for her wise counsel about Hebrew words and phrases;

. . . to Rosemary Keller, former dean at Union, for encouraging me to join the faculty and for supporting me as I moved from parish to academy;

. . . to my colleague Janet Walton for her patience and her impatience in keeping me at this project in the years between the lectures and the book, and to other colleagues in the Arts of Ministry field: Mary Boys, Ana Maria Diaz Stevens, and Ann Ulanov for their unwavering support;

. . . to Robert Seaver, wise mentor and friend, who is thanked in more specific ways in the Preface;

. . . to Bob Ratcliff, Academic Editor at Abingdon Press, for his helpful suggestions for the chapters that frame the lectures, and to Barbara Dick, Production Editor, for her attention to detail on every page of the book;

. . . to Carolina Trevino for diligently tracking down and verifying the quotations in the pages that follow;

. . . to Gladys Moore, Mary Forell, and Janet Peterman, my clergywomen's support group, for the twenty-four years we have met together and for their insistence that I get the book done;

. . . to Pastor Elise Brown, Pastor James Sudbrock, and the people of Advent Lutheran Church for inviting me to be part of the clergy team in that congregation, giving me a place to mark time with a particular community of faith from week to week;

. . . to my family, Nicole and Sam, who have given me their unfailing support and love through the ups and downs of writing and of living.

At the beginning and end of each day, I give thanks to God for marking time with me from the farmlands of Iowa to the streets of New York City. No matter what time it is, God comes, surprising me through words I have heard a hundred times. Mary Oliver's words about poems have taken on special meaning for me: "For poems are not words, after all, but fires for the cold, ropes let down to the lost, something as necessary as bread in the pockets of the hungry. Yes, indeed" (Mary Oliver, *A Poetry Handbook* [New York: Harcourt Brace & Company, 1994], 122). I hope and pray this is true not only of poems, but of sermons. Yes, indeed.

CHAPTER ONE

Marking Time: Reading Scripture at the River's Edge

A t 8:46 a.m. there was silence. No sound on radio or television. No shouting or laughing in the grade school auditorium. No speeches. No taxis honking. The day was September 11, 2003, and New York City was marking time. How long will this go on? Will the silence be broken when the memorial is completed? When Freedom Tower reaches to the sky? When the children sitting in the grade school auditorium have graduated? There are no answers now, only the need to mark time.

"Marking Time" has at least two meanings. When the drum major whistles a certain signal, the marching band comes to a stop. The marchers' feet are still moving up and down, but the band stays in one place. We say they are "marking time." There is another meaning: an intentional attentiveness to the time so that an hour or a day does not pass unnoticed. Someone held in captivity scratches a line on a wall or a stick to mark the rising of the sun, the numbering of the days. The people in the city watch the clock: at 8:46 a.m. they mark the time when the first plane hit the glistening tower on the bluest September day. They etch

1

another mark on their memories, drenched again in sorrow, grateful to be alive one more year.

Throughout the centuries, cultures have developed rituals for marking time: birthing and dying, naming and coming of age. Families celebrate birthdays and circle the dates on the calendar even after loved ones have died. Nations mark the end of a war or its beginning. Religious communities mark time in Sabbaths and seasons. In the church year, even the long season not marked by events in Jesus' life has a name—"Ordinary Time." The longest of the Ten Commandments gathers up both meanings of "marking time." Even as the Hebrew people marked time at the foot of Mount Sinai, God called them to mark their time intentionally with the remembrance of Sabbath:

> Remember the sabbath day, and keep it holy. Six days you shall labor and do all your work. But the seventh day is a sabbath to the LORD your God; you shall not do any work—you, your son or your daughter, your male or female slave, your livestock, or the alien resident in your towns. For in six days the LORD made heaven and earth, the sea, and all that is in them, but rested the seventh day; therefore the LORD blessed the sabbath day and consecrated it. (Exodus 20:8-11)

For those wilderness wanderers, time was to be marked not only by sunrise and sunset but by making a special mark on the stick—a longer mark, a different color—a reminder that God created the days and the nights and all that is in them.

I learned to mark time in a different way during my years as a pastor in the Washington Heights section of Manhattan. In earlier times, this uptown neighborhood on the cliffs above the river was known as "Frankfurt on Hudson" because of the many German Jewish immigrants who settled there during and after World War II. Our church was on Bennett Avenue, an obscure street only eleven blocks long, still home to two Orthodox congregations. On weekday mornings the men rise early for study and prayer at the *yeshiva* before going to work and on the holidays the street is filled with people.

The parish I served shared space with Beth Am, a Reform Jewish congregation. Every Friday night, the music of Sabbath worship drifted up three flights of stairs to my apartment. Over the span of years, I learned to mark time by the rhythm of the Jewish Sabbath. September and October were marked not only by the falling leaves, but by the coming of the new year, Rosh Hashanah. Though I have moved from that street and the apartment above the sanctuary, this rhythm still marks time for me.

The Beecher Lectures that form the core of this book began on the day of Yom Kippur. This timing was coincidental, since convocation at Yale Divinity School was normally scheduled for the second week of October. But as the date approached, my chosen theme of "marking time" intersected the rhythm of these holy days. On the morning of the first lecture, the people of Beth Am had gathered to pray the Yom Kippur liturgy:

> This is the day of awe. What are we, as we stand in Your presence, O God? A leaf in the storm, a fleeting moment in the flow of time, a whisper lost among the stars.
>
> This is the day of decision. Today we invoke You as the Molder of our destiny. Help us to mend the evil of our ways, to right the heart's old wrongs. On this Sabbath of the soul, inscribe us for blessing in the Book of Life.
>
> This is the day of our atonement. We would return to You as penitent children long to return to a loving parent. We confess our sins on this day, knowing that the gates of repentance are always open. Receive us with compassion, and bless us with Your forgiving love.[1]

At the end of the day, the setting sun marked the time when the long day of fasting was broken by sharing a simple meal. The fall cycle of holy days ends with *Simchat Torah* when people dance the scrolls down the aisle of the synagogue and out into the street. On that day, the Jewish people read the last words of Deuteronomy and the first words of Genesis within the same service. The end and the beginning are brought together. Then, for the rest of the year, they unroll the scroll, reading from Genesis toward Deuteronomy, until they arrive once more at the river. No matter that we are almost certain Deuteronomy was written centuries after crossing the Jordan. No matter that we understand the "Books of Moses" as metaphor rather than historical reality. (Hadn't we wondered even in junior high how Moses could have written about his own death?) But in their wisdom the ancient writers returned to that place on the far side of the Jordan. Before crossing over into the new land they stopped. They did not move. They marked time and they listened:

> I call heaven and earth to witness against you today that I have set before you life and death, blessings and curses. Choose life so that you and your descendants may live, loving the LORD your God, obeying [God] . . . so that you may live in the land that the LORD swore to give to your ancestors, to Abraham, to Isaac, and to Jacob. (Deuteronomy 30:19-20)

Every year it is the same. The Jewish people unroll the scroll until they reach the river. Of course they are not the same when they arrive. The same people do not hear the same text in the same way.

In Christian congregations Advent marks the beginning of the church year as the secular year is coming to an end. The Gospel reading for the First Sunday of Advent startles us with words about the last days even as we anticipate Jesus' birth. End and beginning are gathered into one piece. Like Jewish people gathered beside the river, Christian worshipers are not the same as they were a year ago when Advent began. Perhaps for some, there was an empty place at the Thanksgiving table just days before and Christmas seems almost impossible to imagine. The text marks our time, but our time also marks the text. Something will be heard that was not heard a year ago, that was not heard the first time the people stood at the river or when the scroll was read in the time of good King Josiah or when Jesus stood up to read Isaiah's scroll in Nazareth.

Each time we return to the river something has changed, something new is discovered. This is the wonder and urgency of preaching. We may understand this return to the river as the need to make the text relevant to contemporary situations, but there is something more profound going on, something far deeper than finding a new anecdote that will work better now than when we preached this text three years ago. Jewish interpreter Michael Fishbane invites readers to bring their own experiences and questions to the biblical text. Such engagement is not so much a matter of making the text relevant, as it is to gain deeper understanding of the text itself:

> The rhetorical question, "to what does this matter compare?" opens up a hermeneutical space in which similarity is imagined . . . The significance of a similitude is thus that life serves to explain the text, and it gives a concreteness or directness to the text which it might otherwise not have.[2]

When people gathered in New York City churches after the towers had been destroyed, this text from Lamentations was often read:

> How lonely sits the city
>   that once was full of people!
> How like a widow she has become,
>   she that was great among the nations!
> . . . .
> She weeps bitterly in the night,
>   with tears on her cheeks;
> among all her lovers
>   she has no one to comfort her. (Lamentations 1:1-2)

Before September 11, 2001, the reader could understand this poem as a lament over the destruction of Jerusalem. But those who heard this passage of Scripture on the evening of September 11th came to a much deeper understanding of this ancient text. Jerusalem was no longer a biblical city far away in space and time: Jerusalem was now a smoldering heap of ashes and the dust of the towers mingled with the dust of the dead. We had not fully understood the text from Lamentations until that day, but our lives gave "a concreteness or directness to the text," which meant that we heard it and understood it as never before.

"The text lingers," as Walter Brueggemann has said. "Out of that lingering, however, from time to time, words of the text characteristically erupt into new usage. . . . What has been *tradition*, hovering in dormancy, becomes available *experience*."[3]

Marking the Text and Being Marked by It

For centuries, the church has preserved a finite space known as "the canonical Scriptures of the Old and New Testament."[4] Though lively arguments about the boundaries of the canon remain, the sixty-six books of the Bible (plus the Apocrypha in some traditions) have shaped the life of the church since the fourth century. Martin Luther was neither the first nor the last to raise questions about the inclusion of certain books deemed unworthy.[5] Others have protested not what was *included* but what was left out, suspecting that the powers of patriarchy had deleted gospels affirming women. Such debates will no doubt continue, but there is a sense in which the canon can be affirmed as a strange gift and blessing. It is a *strange* gift because even though many "losers" didn't make the final cut, the "winners" are wildly diverse. Tensions remain visible and contradictions unresolved. Two creation stories follow each other with no attempt to harmonize them into one that might make more sense. Miriam's short song is remembered beside Moses' long oratorio in Exodus 15. Jonah and Ruth expand the boundaries of God's beloved people even as Ezra and Esther insist on the peculiar particularity of the people Israel.

Old Testament scholar David Carr celebrates this diversity as a *blessing*, the strange "untamability" of Scripture.[6] Differences and even outright disagreements don't disappear when we move beyond Malachi but may be even more pronounced in the Gospels. Luke's nativity story differs from Matthew's and Mark has no birth story at all. The four stories of Jesus' resurrection all place Mary Magdalene at the tomb, but there are different people at her side in each of the gospels. "Countless harmonizers have attempted to combine these multiple Gospels," says Carr. "Yet the multi-voiced character of the canon stands . . . In sum, untamability is present from the beginning to the end of the Christian canon."[7]

The canon may be closed, but the texts are open. This untamability is a virtue rather than a problem or a threat. Indeed, the problem comes when we try to tame the texts and erase the tensions. Whether we do this by insisting that there is only one static interpretation of a text or by reading all texts through a prescribed doctrinal formula, we wring the life out of the untamable text. Walter Brueggemann warns that this not only muzzles the testimony of the texts but leads to a "thinning of God, the attempt to flatten and refine Yahweh's dense interior. Creedal reductionism does not want to acknowledge this God who leaks out beyond good doctrine. However, the maddening leakage is there in the text, waiting to be spoken of in faith and in dismay."[8]

So it is that when we affirm the biblical canon as "the authoritative source and norm" for our faith and life,[9] we are affirming a book of texts that "leak out" beyond our norms! For preachers and parishioners this means that we do not come to these texts convinced of the correct interpretation nor to discern the one right meaning, but rather to stand on holy ground believing God will meet us there.[10] God is in the tensions within and among texts even as God is present in the tensions and contradictions of our lives. It is the canon itself that has preserved these tensions.

Within the finite boundaries of the canon the texts themselves are not closed, but are open to new hermeneutical insights and possibilities. Every generation, every particular community, hears the texts anew even as former generations wrote these texts out of their own particularities. The texts are marked by the time in which they were written, marked also by editors who reworked the texts at a later time. This marking of the text continues in each generation including our own. For some this may sound like relativism or an undue search for relevance. Rather it is the nature of the texts themselves to be open, untamed, leaking out under our rigid formulations.

Reading Texts in This Time of History

Through most of the long journey of interpreting the Bible there has been a strong conviction that the written text marks the reader. Such an understanding was true when the texts were taken literally as dictated by God. When the literal meaning was obscure, it was the text's allegorical meaning that marked the reader or the hearer. In later years, an enlightenment approach to the text as historical document meant that the text could be understood rationally. But even this rational meaning continued to mark the reader.

In recent years more attention has been paid to how the reader marks the text. Every reader comes to the text from a particular social location that determines how the text is heard and interpreted. Objectivity is an illusion that denies the role of the reader, whether that reader is an untrained layperson or a tenured biblical professor. Subjective approaches such as reader response theory have suggested that texts have no meaning other than that brought by each individual. Without saying the text has disappeared, such approaches have opened the way for readers to have a bigger role in discerning the meaning of biblical texts.

New Testament scholar Vincent Wimbush sometimes startles students by telling them the Bible is a modern book. While they protest that the Bible was written long before they stepped into class, Wimbush nudges them to see that each generation reads the text in new ways and, in that sense, creates a new book. He lifts up the experience of African people in the United States as one example. In the late eighteenth century African Americans became familiar with the Bible through evangelical camp meetings. They were drawn to the vivid stories, even when those stories were read by white people, including their masters:

> What did not go unnoticed among the Africans was the fact that the white world they experienced tended to explain its power and authority by appeal to the Bible. So they embraced the Bible, transforming it from the book of the religion of the

whites . . . into a language world of strong hopes and veiled but stinging critique of slave-holding Christian culture.[11]

From his own experience and his research, Wimbush then asks an intriguing question: "How does a people enslaved by a people of a Book come to accept that Book as authoritative and legitimate?"[12] He finds the answer in a "meeting of worlds." African-Americans' experience of slavery and survival met the world of the Bible where God led Hebrew slaves to freedom and where a Savior, who was as harshly treated as they were, ultimately triumphed. Obviously, the white slave masters had read the Bible from a very different social location, a radically different particularity. For African Americans the Bible "changed from 'text'— understood as static source of eternal truth . . . to a language world that could easily, freely, with much creative play, be engaged 'from below,' or from the margins."[13] Such a "meeting of worlds" has elicited new readings of biblical texts in Latin American base communities and in the Circle of African Women Theologians. Biblical texts have found new meaning in church basements where African-American women have seen reflections of their own lives in the story of Hagar and her son Ishmael. Gay and lesbian communities have seen themselves sitting at Jesus' expansive banquet table and have heard echoes of their own commitments in the lifelong covenant between David and Jonathan. These communities have brought their own lives into conversation with the open, untamable text. They have marked the text in new ways.

Yet the text itself remains an essential partner in these conversations. The reader is not the measure of everything for the text continues to have a voice. New Testament scholar Adele Berlin urges a middle ground between objective and subjective extremes. She acknowledges that few people today insist that a text has only one meaning or that any of us can be completely objective in our reading. Yet she speaks up on behalf of the text itself when she says, ". . . it could be argued that just as no reading is free of input from the reader, so no reading is free of input from the text."[14]

Thus, in her interpretive work, Berlin draws us deeply into the text itself, looking for repeated words, patterns, and unusual constructions. Then, she selects the features that will be important for interpretation, acknowledging that such selection is always a subjective process. Readers will differ in choosing which features are most important, but whatever features are chosen, they can be said to reside in the text. Finally, she moves to a third step: deciding what to do with the features selected and how to make sense of them.[15] Other interpreters might choose a different process, but what is clear in Berlin's approach is that the biblical text itself has a voice, a voice as genuine and particular as the voice of the reader. Not only does our time mark the text, but the text marks our time—and us.

Marking Time—A Matter of Faith

Issues of objectivity and subjectivity can be applied to interpreting any piece of literature. However, it is *faith* that claims the Bible as the "Word of God," different from Shakespeare's *Hamlet* or even Dante's *Divine Comedy*. Sandra Schneiders points to this distinction in her book *The Revelatory Text*:

> From one point of view, the biblical text is a human text, and one can develop a hermeneutical theory that will ground its interpretation as a human text. Such a theory would be substantially identical with the hermeneutical theory developed for the interpretation of any classical religious text. From another point of view . . . this text is sacred scripture, and an adequate hermeneutical theory is one that takes full account of the Bible's reality as a human text that is a privileged mediation of the divine-human encounter.[16]

To say that the Bible is a "mediation of the divine-human encounter" is itself a faith statement. Such an encounter moves us to take off our shoes—even though we no longer think that Moses wrote the Pentateuch. This understanding of the Bible as holy ground is rooted in religious communities that have shaped the biblical texts and continue to be shaped by them. Even when people have wildly different opinions about the authority of the Bible, the very notion that they debate the matter has something to do with God.

For people in Christian communities the Bible functions as a kind of family album.[17] We leaf through the Bible looking at the odd photographs of our ancestors. There they are—wearing strange clothes and speaking in ways we no longer recognize. Like some of our personal family albums, there are pictures we would rather not talk about: the vengeful, bloody conquests of the people of Canaan; the deadly irony of Jephthah's daughter running out to meet her father after his victory in battle; the oppressive commands for women to keep silence; the permissive attitudes toward human slavery. Yet we also see pictures that give life to us and offer meaning when other stories fail. When we open the Bible we realize that faith in God did not begin with us. The pictures now yellowed with age were pasted into the book by others who longed to be in communion with God, who tried to discern how God wanted them to live with their neighbors. While Christians affirm that Jesus as the "Word of God" is not reducible to print on a page, we would know little or nothing about Jesus without the pictures pasted in the book.

This family album was stitched together over centuries of time, yet through all the pages, there is a sense that the writers were moved by a divine-human encounter: a burning bush, golden cherubim in the temple suddenly coming to life, the heavens torn apart at Jesus' baptism, the Spirit poured out on all flesh at Pentecost. Of course all of these statements are faith statements rather than products of literary analysis. While it is possible to analyze biblical texts using historical, sociological, and rhetorical tools, it is not possible to discern the full meaning of these texts without faith. "Faith as a fundamental openness to the religious truth claims of the text is a requirement for even minimally valid interpretation of the text as *text*; faith as thematic Christian commitment is necessary for interpretation of the Bible as *scripture*."[18]

It is faith that hears Scripture as God's "living word" and, if living, this word continues to be revelatory in every generation. The untamable text remains open to new interpretations, flexible enough to engender a "meeting of worlds" in very different times within and among diverse communities. The texts that came into being through people of faith carry the seeds of meaning into the present and move into the future. If we believe the Bible is God's living word, then the full meaning of the texts is still being revealed. From this perspective, preaching is a continuation of the text's witness. For James Nieman this is a different way of framing the question of how Scripture relates to preaching than what he calls "the stock American Protestant answer":

> In that view, preaching needs scripture in order to ground its claims and confer authority. By contrast, an ecclesiological perspective on the question indicates that *scripture needs preaching* so that the resources and hope of earlier generations is brought to bear in a critical fashion for the church's mission today.[19]

To say "scripture needs preaching" is to believe that the text not only marks our time, but our time also marks the text. "Preaching is biblical when it extends the open word of scripture and particularizes it anew for the sake of declaring God's desire for life."[20]

Marking Time: Sermon as Meeting Place

For preachers, this third millennium can be an exhilarating time. The biblical text has been given back to us with its wild untamability intact. Preachers are invited to let the words of the text speak to them without an unrelenting skepticism that the "real" meaning lies hidden in an oral prehistory. The gifts of historical criticism are not set aside, but neither are they assumed to be the only lens through which to read the words on the page. Surprise and delight are encouraged as the reader pays attention to odd details within the texture of the text. Doctrinal formulations are not abandoned but the preacher has the audacity to listen for a word that leaks out under confessions and creeds. The role of the reader is acknowledged in ways that affirm approaching the text in faith as a "living word." The text is subject and the reader is subject, and the two are in conversation with each other. Thus, the sermon is a meeting place between the Scripture text and the community text. Each text has a unique voice. Both the Scripture text and the community text must be exegeted with attentiveness and care, not in order to be "relevant" but in order to hear God's living word in its depth and particularity.

How does marking time shape our preaching? Hopefully, such an understanding of the interplay between text and time will energize and enliven our engagement with the Scripture texts themselves. As preachers we will be more confident in bringing insights from our own particular time into conversation with the texts and we will invite the congregation to do the same. The sermon does more than *apply* an ancient text to a contemporary setting as though the conversation goes only one way. Our experiences in this time of history also mark the text and we understand the text in a way that is different from any interpretation in the past. There may even be passages we could not have understood until the present time. Did we New Yorkers understand Lamentations 1 before the devastation of 9/11? Did American Christians have any idea what Exodus meant before African slaves sang the story out of their own experience of oppression? Did I grasp the meaning of Psalm 23 before I walked through the cemetery after saying the benediction over my father's coffin?

How might we prepare a sermon from the perspective of marking time? Imagine that the Scripture text is the familiar story of Jesus feeding the five thousand in Matthew 14:13-21, a story found in some form in all four Gospels. The text has its own unique voice and we need to let it speak fully on its own terms. You might ask a member of the congregation to read the text aloud to you—then write your response without stopping or censoring. Over a year's time, fifty different members of the congregation

13

could be engaged as readers and feel more of a stake in the sermon itself. If this seems too difficult, read the text from a Bible without any notes or underlining, trying to hear the text as you've never heard it before. Walk around and let your body respond. Where did you walk faster or slower or come to a full stop? How did you feel in the midst of this great crowd? Why the little after-thought about "women and children"? How many would there have been if the women and children were counted? Pay close attention to the texture of the text, looking for repetitions, patterns, or contrasts. This is a deserted place, yet there is great abundance—for "all ate and were filled." There's an opposition between the words *deserted* and *filled*.

The beginning of this passage won't let us stay within the boundaries of the appointed verses: "Now when Jesus heard this, he withdrew from there . . ." Such an opening line always points us to what came before we entered the story. What did Jesus hear that made him withdraw? We go back to the previous verses and discover another banquet—Herod's birthday dinner. This meal is not in a deserted place but in the king's palace. There isn't a great crowd, but a guest list limited to a chosen few. Were there abundant baskets of food left over after Herod's guests were fed? There was only one horrible leftover: the head of John the Baptist served on a platter. Two very different banquets placed side by side in Matthew's gospel, but we seldom hear these stories together.

How does our time mark this text and how do the contrasting stories of the larger text mark our time? There are deserted places in our communities, in our country, and in the larger world: what do these deserted places look like and how do they help us see and hear Matthew's story? Where do we see the contrasts between "deserted" and "filled" where we live? The pictures may be close at hand: the line around the block at the food pantry or senior citizens making choices between needed prescriptions and groceries. Newspaper stories and photographs take us beyond our immediate neighborhood to the Ninth Ward of New Orleans or a mother and child waiting for U.N. food relief in the refugee camps of Darfur. Surely there are five thousand longing to be fed—"besides women and children."

The text also marks our time, for these side-by-side stories challenge us not only to observe but also to respond. We have seen other banquets in our community, in our country, and in the larger world—tables heaped high with lavish mounds of food and the deadly cost of protecting wealth and power. Is Herod only an evil villain or captive to imperial arrangements he refused to challenge? Where do we see Herod's banquet serving nothing but deadly leftovers? Do the priorities of Empire, whether ancient or modern, crowd out Jesus' abundant banquet? In spite of these overwhelming and often depressing questions, Jesus comes into our time with words of challenge and hope: "They need not go away; you give them something to eat." The sermon begins to take shape out of this lively conversation: our time marks the text of these two very different banquets and the text marks our time with urgent challenge and irrepressible hope.

Three Biblical Texts as Conversation Partners

The chapters that follow offer models for listening attentively to three different Scripture passages in order to discern how each text marks our time and how our time marks each text. The interplay of text and time varies from one chapter to another. In some cases, the text appears to be static or timeless, giving our own time no permission to enter. In other cases, our time marks the text so heavily with skepticism that we dismiss the text as completely naïve or irrelevant. We don't allow the text to mark our time at all. Sometimes rehearsing the interpretive history of a text becomes a guide to new understandings in the present. Engaging these three texts can open up new possibilities for reading other passages of Scripture so that the lingering texts can explode with meaning, marking time with those who speak and those who listen.

Chapter 2 turns to a story that never appears in the Christian lectionary. This long, detailed story of the Shunammite woman in 2 Kings 4 has suffered not only from neglect but also from a double misfortune if it is read at all: a formulaic understanding that names it simply as part of the "Elijah/Elisha cycle" or a feminist deconstruction that dismisses the story as one more instance of patriarchal propaganda. What happens when we honor the wild untamability of the text? What do we discover when we listen closely to the stubborn woman in the story, even as we acknowledge the validity of the feminist critique? What happens when we pay attention to where the story has been placed within the boundaries of the canon? How does our time mark the text? What voices have we heard that connect our lives with the stubborn Shunammite woman and her persistence in saving her little son?

The story of Jesus' encounter with a rich man is the focus of chapter 3. Unlike the text from 2 Kings, this familiar story is heard in some form almost every year in the lectionary cycle of readings. This text does not suffer from a lack of exposure but from our need to distance ourselves from Jesus' difficult words. Each time of history has marked this text as impossible—from the protests of Jesus' disciples to the present time marked by excessive consumerism and greed. Our discomfort talking about money can distance us from this text, and it is not unusual for scholarly commentaries to increase the distance. In this time of complex economic arrangements, this text is seen as completely unrealistic, naïve, and even dangerous.

How do we preach a text we don't want to be in? Is it possible for this text to mark our time in any way? What does it mean for Christian people to stand with the rich man or with the disciples? How does this text call into question the assumptions of our present age? How do we help people move beyond guilt and defensiveness that often drive them away from this text and away from Jesus?

Chapter 4 takes us to Acts 8 as the Jesus movement expands beyond Jerusalem into Samaria and to the ends of the earth. The Ethiopian eunuch in this story is more familiar than the Shunammite woman of 2 Kings 4, but the story is heard only once every three years in the lectionary cycle of readings. We read this text on one of the Sundays after Easter, the season when the First Reading always comes from the book of Acts. There is no reading from the First/Old Testament; yet understanding this text depends on a lively *conversational circle* between the two testaments.[21] This conversation between the two testaments can be as life giving as Philip interpreting the scroll of Isaiah in the chariot. In hearing this text it is essential to consider the interplay between Luke's time, Isaiah's time, and our own time. What is the significance of the word *Ethiopian* and the word *eunuch?* What resources beyond the text itself are needed to understand these terms? How did Luke's understanding of these terms mark the text? How might a conversational circle between Acts and Isaiah open our eyes to new possibilities for interpreting not only this text but also other passages in Scripture? Who is like the Ethiopian eunuch in our own time of history? What happens when we discover that Philip had to depend on something more than the words written down?

Questions such as these will be explored more deeply in the pages that follow. Like our ancestors in faith, we return once more to the river. The texts linger as they have for generations. We come to the river as different people than we were the last time the story was read. How does the text mark our time? How does our time mark the text? Preaching at the river's edge calls us to be attentive to both of these questions.

CHAPTER TWO

It Will Be All Right: New Rubrics for the Holy Man's Room

The text lingers . . . Out of that lingering, however, from time to time, words of the text characteristically erupt into new usage . . . What has been tradition, hovering in dormancy, becomes available experience.[1]

We turn now to such a lingering text, a text I had forgotten or missed entirely until a long-ago conversation with my colleague Rabbi Margaret Moers Wenig. During the years when we shared a common worship space, she became my rabbi. She introduced me to texts I had missed in my recurring three-year journey through the lectionary. One day she invited me into this story in 2 Kings, chapter 4:

> One day Elisha was passing through Shunem, where a wealthy woman lived, who urged him to have a meal. So whenever he passed that way, he would stop there for a meal. She said to her husband, "Look, I am sure that this man who regularly passes our way is a holy man of God. Let us make a small roof chamber with walls, and put there for him a bed, a table, a chair, and a lamp, so that he can stay there whenever he comes to us."

One day when [Elisha] came there, he went up to the chamber and lay down there. He said to his servant Gehazi, "Call the Shunammite woman." When he had called her, she stood before him. He said to him, "Say to her, Since you have taken all this trouble for us, what may be done for you? Would you have a word spoken on your behalf to the king or to the commander of the army?" She answered, "I live among my own people." He said, "What then may be done for her?" Gehazi answered, "Well, she has no son, and her husband is old." He said, "Call her." When he had called her, she stood at the door. He said, "At this season, in due time, you shall embrace a son." She replied, "No, my lord, O man of God; do not deceive your servant."

The woman conceived and bore a son at that season, in due time, as Elisha had declared to her.

When the child was older, he went out one day to his father among the reapers. He complained to his father, "Oh, my head, my head!" The father said to his servant, "Carry him to his mother." He carried him and brought him to his mother; the child sat on her lap until noon, and he died. She went up and laid him on the bed of the man of God, closed the door on him, and left. Then she called to her husband, and said, "Send me one of the servants and one of the donkeys, so that I may quickly go to the man of God and come back again." He said, "Why go to him today? It is neither new moon nor sabbath." She said, "It will be all right." Then she saddled the donkey and said to her servant, "Urge the animal on; do not hold back for me unless I tell you." So she set out, and came to the man of God at Mount Carmel.

When the man of God saw her coming, he said to Gehazi his servant, "Look, there is the Shunammite woman; run at once to meet her, and say to her, Are you all right? Is your husband all right? Is the child all right?" She answered, "It is all right." When she came to the man of God at the mountain, she caught hold of his feet. Gehazi approached to push her away. But the man of God said, "Let her alone, for she is in bitter distress; the LORD has hidden it from me and has not told me." Then she said, "Did I ask my lord for a son? Did I not say, Do not mislead me?" He said to Gehazi, "Gird up your loins, and take my staff in your hand, and go. If you meet anyone, give no greeting, and if anyone greets you, do not answer; and lay my staff on the face of the child." Then the mother of the child said, "As the LORD lives, and as you yourself live, I will not leave without you." So he rose up and followed her. Gehazi went on ahead and laid the staff on the face of the child, but there was no sound or sign of life. He came back to meet him and told him, "The child has not awakened."

When Elisha came into the house, he saw the child lying dead on his bed. So he went in and closed the door on the two of them, and prayed to the LORD. Then he got up on the bed and lay upon the child, putting his mouth upon his mouth, his eyes upon his eyes, and his hands upon his hands; and while he lay bent over him, the flesh of the child became warm. He got down, walked once to and fro in the room, then got up again and bent over him; the child sneezed seven times, and the child opened his eyes. Elisha summoned Gehazi and said, "Call the Shunammite woman." So he called her. When she came to him, he said, "Take your son." She came and fell at his feet bowing to the ground; then she took her son and left. (2 Kings 4:8-37)

How has this story been heard at the river's edge? For generations, it was gathered up with other stories in chapter 4 under titles such as "Elisha's Wondrous Deeds."[2] Sometimes, it was placed within the larger context of 1 and 2 Kings as part of "The Elijah–Elisha Cycle." A quick review of commentaries reveals what has been heard:

- The story compares and contrasts Elijah and Elisha, showing both continuity and discontinuity between the two.[3]
- Second Kings, chapter 4, echoes 1 Kings, chapter 17: both have stories of women and overflowing jars of oil. Both move on with stories of an only son raised from death with Elisha following the rubrics of his mentor Elijah.
- Going beyond the Old Testament, interpreters have noted patterns picked up by Mark, Luke, and John: "The pivotal relationship . . . between John and Jesus has a perfect counterpart in the relationship between Elijah and Elisha."[4]

Elisha's name—like the name Jesus—means "the one who saves."

But one day, when we returned to the river, we noticed the Shunammite woman. It did not just happen. Women found her languishing in the text, a neglected human prop for Elisha's magical miracle tour. It's easy to forget how much biblical scholarship has changed in the last twenty-five years. Many books by feminist biblical scholars now considered "classics" have been written since I started seminary in 1976.[5] It was in 1978 that Phyllis Trible urged us to turn to the biblical texts with the tenacity of the woman searching for one lost coin.[6] So it was that women combed the concordance and peered under the rug that had covered up countless women. They brought these women into the light of day—including many whose names had been forgotten. But the celebration was short-lived, as short as the life of the little boy who died at noon on his mother's lap. It soon became apparent that the biblical stories giving most attention to women often turned out to be the most patriarchal of all. Suspicion replaced rejoicing. It wasn't yet time to call in the neighbors to say, "Look what we've found!"

It is not difficult to unmask this story; after all, its patriarchal priorities are not well hidden.[7] Elisha can't even talk to this woman. She stands before him in the room she has made for him. While we're waiting to see what Elisha will say to her, the text reads, "He said to him…" He said to *him*? What's going on here? Elisha seems a strange ventriloquist, putting words into the mouth of Gehazi, his servant. Was it beneath Elisha to speak directly to this woman? After all Elisha seems a man of some status—he has connections with the king and the commander of the army. "Shall I offer a word on her behalf?" he dictates to Gehazi.

"I live among my own people," she says. I don't need your help, she implies. But she gave the wrong answer. Gehazi knows better. "Well," he says to his master, "she has no son, and her husband is old." There it is. No matter what she thinks she does not need, she needs a son. "Call her again," Elisha says, though it is not clear when she left. When she returns she doesn't come in but stands at the door. Has she become suspicious of what the holy man might say? This time Elisha speaks directly to her: "At this season, in due time, you shall embrace a son."

"No, my lord, O man of God: do not deceive your servant." Elisha never responds. Her pleading protest hangs in the air. The story moves on as though she hadn't said a thing: "The woman conceived and bore a son at that season, in due time, as Elisha has declared to her." Elisha speaks directly to her only two times: once to tell her she will embrace a son and finally to say, "Take your son." He has no way of relating to her except as a mother. Once more a woman without a name (the Shunammite woman) follows another woman without a name (the widow of Zarapheth)—both of them mothers intent on saving their sons.

Woman-as-mother is essential, but also threatening. Thus it is the holy men who become the *real* life-givers, Elijah first and then Elisha. Over against the primordial power of pregnancy and birth, the holy man alone claims the power to renew life, to revive the child. In the church this life-giving power extends to baptism. The Lutheran baptismal rite begins with these words: ". . . We are born children of a fallen humanity; in the waters of Baptism we are reborn children of God and inheritors of eternal life."[8] Birth from a woman is part of our fallen human state and leads to death. But baptism does what our fallen birth can never do, granting eternal life beyond death "in the name of the Father, and of the Son and of the Holy Spirit." Every woman should be a mother but as a mother she can never do what the Father can.

Whether focusing only on Elisha's wondrous deeds or unmasking the patriarchal project of this story, the woman of Shunem disappears. She is no more.

But now we come to the river once again. Patrocinio Schweickart poses a perplexing question: "Why," she asks, "do some (not all) demonstrably sexist texts remain appealing even after they have been subjected to thorough feminist critique?"[9] Why, we ask, does this unnamed woman beckon us into the story even after it has been unmasked?

The text lingers. Biblical scholars like Phyllis Trible and Walter Brueggemann have urged us to pay closer attention to the text itself. Why such details if the writers simply wanted to show continuity or contrast between Elijah and Elisha? Why such a strong and feisty woman who threatens to steal the show all together? While we've often heard that "the devil is in the details," perhaps God is in the details and we had not been paying attention.[10]

We need to take a closer look. The Shunammite woman is *gedolah*, translated here as "wealthy."[11] But that Hebrew word can also mean "great," as in the next chapter: "Naaman, commander of the army of the king of Aram, was a *great* man . . ." (italics added). Is she here in chapter 4 as a counterpart to Naaman the warrior? The text doesn't tell us such things. But it does tell us she is a woman who knows holiness when she sees it. She is sure Elisha is a "holy man of God" and she wants to be close to holiness. Sharing a meal is not enough so she builds a small chamber for him to be in residence: a bed, a table, a chair, and a lamp. The details mark the place so we cannot forget it. Is this room in her house as holy as the holy man's mountain?

The narrator does not tell us if the woman laughed for joy like Sarah when her son was born. All too quickly the story moves toward sadness. The details are poignant, wrenching. "Oh, my head, my head!" cries the little lad. Like Elisha, the father calls for his servant: "Carry the boy to his mother." Surely she will know what to do, but all she can do is embrace him on her lap, hold him until noon, and then he dies.

Why does she lay him on the holy man's bed? Has that room become a kind of shrine—when she opens the door again will he be sitting up very much alive? She insists on a connection between the holy man and her son—she will not let Elisha forget. She will not accept her son's death even though she never asked for his birth. She takes charge, giving orders to her husband. Get the servants! Saddle the donkeys! The text speeds up, but her husband stops the action: "Why go to the holy man today? It is neither new moon nor Sabbath." Did he even ask, "How is the lad?" Does he wonder if there was any connection between her untimely trip and the boy? He offers this pragmatic question: "Why go to him today? It is neither new moon nor Sabbath." A footnote in the *New Oxford Annotated Bible* explains: "It was considered more propitious to visit a prophet on holy days."[12]

"It will be all right," is all she says. *Shalom* is the word in Hebrew. *Shalom*, the expansive and elusive word. *Shalom*: it is well. *Shalom*: peace to you. *Shalom*: good-bye, I'm leaving! She heeds neither her husband nor the footnote. For her, this *is* a propitious time. "It will be all right," she says. Does she believe it?

When she comes near Mount Carmel, Elisha sees her coming. Evidently he has not changed since the earlier part of the story. He is the model of executive leadership, delegating duties, dictating what Gehazi should say to the woman: "Are you all right?" (*Ha-Shalom*—Have you *shalom?*) Is your husband all right?"

Oh, Elisha, stop. We cannot bear the next question. Please stop. "Is the child all right?"

"It is all right," she says. *Shalom*—though there is none.

With that word she rushes past Gehazi as quickly as she had left her husband. No memo will do. No excuse about the moon or his calendar being full. No more distance. No standing in the doorway. She pushes on until she is close enough to catch hold of Elisha's feet. Gehazi knows the rubrics and tries to push her away. She has come at a most unpropitious time.

But now Elisha sees her, not far off, but close at hand. "Let her alone," he says, "for she is in bitter distress; the LORD has hidden it from me and has not told me." Elisha is an imperfect holy man. He misses things, words, signs. Perhaps he hadn't listened to God any better than he had listened to the woman. But now Elisha sees her embracing the empty place where her son had been. The truth once hidden is revealed in her body. "Did I ask for a son? Did I not say, do not mislead me?" What can the holy man say? There is no message to dictate, no way to escape her question. But he had not deceived her. She had given birth in due season. That was the end of it for him, but not for her. Her son is lying on the holy man's bed. She will not let him forget his connection to the child. Nor will she let him forget who he is: he is the holy man of God. Surely, now, he will do something.

He sends his servant! Is this all Elisha can manage—to send his staff with his staff? These rubrics have worked before: the staff turned squirming snake in Pharaoh's court, the staff parting the waters of the sea, Elijah's mantle rolled up like a staff making a path through the Jordan and Elisha repeating the action to make sure he could do it too! This is no ordinary stick anymore than a bishop's crosier can be called a stick. It is a sign of the holy man's office, the holy man's power: "Go, lay it upon the face of the child."

Oh no, this will not do, not for the Great Woman. This is not *shalom*. "As the LORD lives and as you yourself live, I will not leave you." She echoes Elisha's own words, his oath spoken three times to his mentor Elijah (2 Kings 2:2, 4, 6). Do the words tumble around inside his head beckoning memory and finally action? Like the persistent widow knocking on the judge's door in Jesus' parable, this woman cannot be dismissed. She is the one who makes things happen. She has spoken: "It will be all right." At her insistence Elisha finally leaves his mountain. But soon it becomes clear that it is not all right. The old rubrics have not worked. Gehazi bears the bad news: "The child has not awakened." But Elisha doesn't turn around on the road.

The holy man seems utterly alone as this last scene begins. He goes into the house, up the stairs to the familiar room—the table, the chair, the lamp, and the bed—just as he remembered it. Except for one thing: the little boy lying still. His staff was useless. He closes the door, just the two of them now. What can he do but pray? He gets up on the bed. Gone is every notion of propriety. Gone, too, is the distance between holy man and child: he puts his own body where his crosier had been. His mouth on the child's mouth, eyes upon his eyes, hands upon his hands. The boy's flesh grows warm, but it is not yet *shalom*. He walks around the room, touching the lamp, the chair, the table. One more time he bends over the boy (though for Elijah it had worked the first time). Don't try too hard to discern if this is an early reference to artificial respiration. Instead, listen: the boy sneezes seven times and opens his eyes! What a wondrously undignified conclusion, that sneezing. What an odd liturgical sound in the holy man's room.

Elisha has become more than a magician. He has moved from distance to closeness, a flawed but faithful man of

God. And the unnamed Shunammite woman is far more complex than a prop or a victim of patriarchal propaganda. She has pushed her way through every attempt to discount her. Like Elisha on Mount Carmel, we finally see her.

But still there is more. For our time marks the text bringing insights even the writers could not imagine. Recall Michael Fishbane's claim in *The Exegetical Imagination:*

> The rhetorical question, "to what does this matter compare?" opens up a hermeneutical space in which similarity is imagined . . . The significance of a similitude is thus that life serves to explain the text, and it gives a concreteness or directness to the text which it might otherwise not have.[13]

In preaching we ask not only what is in the text but also what does this community bring to the text? For preachers, this dense, detailed text is rich with possibilities when we search for the "similitudes" between the text and our own time.

Who is like her, loving holiness? She is not like everybody. There are limits within the text: we cannot make her a poor widow or a foreigner or a feminist. But I think we have seen a "similitude": the women who gave their "egg money" to help build churches on the prairies, the women's auxiliary who darned the socks of the pre-seminary students at Luther College.[14] You may have your own stories of women who built those rooms: a bed, a table, a chair, a lamp. These women could be close to holiness, but not too close—unclean for centuries, unfit, uneducated, unlike-the-disciples. Like her latter-day sisters, Mary and Martha, *Gedolah* invites a holy man to eat with her. It isn't only about food even as the room isn't only about shelter. "I have a part in holiness," she says.

Where have we seen her persistence? Her husband's question has been repeated a thousand times through the ages: "Why go to him today? It is neither new moon nor Sabbath." Her sisters have heard those words more times than they can count. Not now, woman, the church is not ready. Not now, it's too divisive. Not now: this is the year for evangelism or stewardship or whatever.

Not now—we already have two women on the faculty! It's not only her sisters who have heard that question but also anyone who dared to challenge propitious timing. So it was that Dr. King wrote to his brother white clergy from the Birmingham jail:

> For years now I have heard the word "Wait!" It rings in the ear of every Negro with piercing familiarity. This "Wait" has almost always meant "Never." We must come to see, with one of our distinguished jurists, that "justice too long delayed is justice denied."[15]

The Shunammite woman comes today to encourage us to "keep on keeping on" even when many insist that the time is not right.

What does she want now? We can never know if she wanted a son, but once her son was born, she wanted to embrace him far past noon. Becoming a mother shaped her even as building Elisha's room shaped her. Mothering isn't everything, but it surely isn't nothing. Womanist theologian Delores Williams challenges her white sisters to do more than unmask biblical stories, even as she challenges her African-American brothers to be attentive to the lives of black women. For Williams, Hagar and Ishmael's wilderness journey becomes the counterpoint to the Exodus story so central in black liberation theology. Liberation cannot disregard survival and quality of life. Williams did not learn this from the commentaries, but in the company of African-American women conversing with Hagar in countless church basements.[16]

The Shunammite woman is not an oppressed slave or a poor widow. But we need not turn her into something she is not to imagine her joining hands with Hagar and the widow of Zarapheth, doing whatever is necessary to ensure survival for her child. She is a *Shalom*-maker. She refuses to believe that embracing her son was meant to be so short-lived. Have we seen her? Has the church seen her or have we been too distant, staying up on our holy mountains? Heidi Neumark has been pastor in the South Bronx for fifteen years; she has seen her often:

Recently in the Bronx, 4 year old Pedro's mother was afraid to take him to the emergency room and risk deportation because it is now legal for hospital workers to report on the immigration status of patients. By the time his desperate mother decided she couldn't lower his fever and she risked the hospital, it was too late. Pedro died within the hour, for want of simple antibiotics.[17]

Holiness and *shalom* must be held together. Elisha cannot tell this woman to bear a child whether by miracle or choice, slavery or rape, then go back to his mountain or his monastery, sanctuary or seminary. The rubrics of *shalom* are far different. He cannot send his servant or his crosier: he must get as close to the boy as his own breathing.

What about her husband? Does *shalom* have anything to do with him? Compared to the rich details that give life to his wife, he seems an uncaring cardboard figure. He doesn't carry the boy home, doesn't leave his work, doesn't ask how the boy is, doesn't wonder what to do if she leaves the house. All he can do is suggest how foolish she is for going to the holy man at the wrong time. Must we leave the story there or can we speak to the gaps and the silences in the text?

Barton Sutter marks our time in a poem based on a true story from the great Chicago snowstorm of 1979, a poem called "The Snowman":

> This is a poem for Tom.
> This is a poem for Tom Blair.
> This is a poem for him
> And for all of the men on the edge
> Of their beds in their underwear,
> Wondering what they're doing there.
> This is a poem for them.
> For all of the good providers.
> . . . .
> Thomas Blair drove a plow,
> And because of the snow in '79
> He worked a lot of overtime.

Not that I blame the snow.
But because of the snow
The work was there,
And there was the wife and kid,
A regular blizzard of debts, and so
The food of the poem is coffee,
Coffee and cigarettes.

Tom went to work
And he worked and worked,
With little time off,
And he worked and worked,
And one day, Tom,
He went berserk.
He forgot all about the snow
And started plowing up cars,
And some had people in them,
And some of the people died.

Can you see the blue lights of his truck?
The cherrytops of the cops?
He wrecked forty cars with the plow
Before they got him stopped,
And when they could hear
What the screaming said,
You know what the screaming said?
"*I hate my job!*
I want to see my kid!
I hate my goddamned job!"

So that's it. That's the poem.
What do you think?
What do you think it's all about?
It's not about the snow
So much as . . . I'll tell you
What it's about.
This is a poem for Tom.
This is a poem for Tom Blair.
This is a poem for him
And for all of the men on the edge

Of their beds in their underwear,
Wondering what they're doing there.
This is a poem for them.
For all of the good providers.[18]

Can we open a hermeneutical space for the father? Can he learn new rubrics, come closer, and in due season embrace his child? Genuine *shalom* changes not only the lives of women and children but also the lives of men. *Shalom* is the song Mary sang of a world turned upside down transforming not only those who are poor and hungry, but also those who are rich and well fed (Luke 1:46-55).

Where Is God?

God is in both texts, the Scripture text and the community text. Through the testimony of the text, God's living word speaks to us across the centuries into the present time. The text marks our time. But our time also marks the text, for the testimony of the community changes how the text is heard—the testimony of poor women in the South Bronx, the testimony of Dr. King in the Birmingham jail, the testimony of black women who insist on survival and well-being against the legacy of slavery, the testimony of the anguished father screaming from the snow plow. Their testimonies change not only how we hear the text but also how we hear and speak of God.

I asked Rabbi Wenig, "When do you read this text?" She opened her book to find the place. "It's the *haftarah* reading appointed alongside Genesis 18 through 22." For a moment she was silent. "Isaac," she said. "The Genesis reading ends with the sacrifice of Isaac." Could the story of the Shunammite woman be a *midrash* on Genesis 18–22? Both stories begin with hospitality to holiness. Abraham invites three holy messengers to stay and eat. *Gedolah* invites the holy man to eat and stay. The holy strangers make a promise to Abraham: "I will surely return to you in due season, and your wife Sarah shall have a son"—almost the same words Elisha speaks to the Shunammite woman. Indeed, the Hebrew *ka'et hayya* is found only in these two places.[19] Miraculously, both sons survive—one through the intervention of an angel, the other through the stubborn intervention of his mother. Abraham's obedience to God in offering his son is reckoned as righteousness. Was *Gedolah's* stubborn cry for *shalom* also reckoned as righteousness?

If we had put the near sacrifice of Isaac behind us, the text will not let us forget. Second Kings 3 ends with the king of Moab surrounded by the troops of Israel and Judah in holy war. Desperate, the Moabite king "took his firstborn son who was to succeed him, and offered him as a burnt offering on the wall. And great wrath came upon Israel, so they withdrew from him and returned to their own land" (2 Kings 3:27). Chapter 4 interrupts these holy wars. *Shalom* will not be sacrificed. This chapter, set down between a war and a great warrior, portrays the fullness of *shalom*: debts repaid with overflowing vessels of oil, a son restored to life on the holy man's bed, a pot of poisoned stew made edible, and barley loaves enough to feed a hundred—with some left over (2 Kings 4:1-44)!

So what do you think? Can all of this be explained by scribal redaction? Or did God have something to do with it—surprising even the editors and scribes? The Great Woman of Shunem comes. "*Shalom*," she says, even when there is none: *Shalom* for Hagar and Ishmael setting off into the wilderness. *Shalom* for the little boy who dies too soon on his mother's lap. *Shalom* for Pedro's mother in the South Bronx. *Shalom* for the father sitting on the edge of his bed wondering what he's doing there. Today *Gedolah* comes to the river. Unordained. Holy. Daring to speak the words of a priest:

> May God bless you and keep you,
> May God's face shine upon you and be gracious unto you,
> May God look upon you with favor
> And give you—
> *Shalom*. (Numbers 6:24-26)

CHAPTER THREE

The Camel and the Cash Machine: A Story We Try to Forget

As [Jesus] was setting out on a journey, a man ran up and knelt before him, and asked him, "Good Teacher, what must I do to inherit eternal life?" Jesus said to him, "Why do you call me good? No one is good but God alone. You know the commandments: 'You shall not murder; You shall not commit adultery; You shall not steal; You shall not bear false witness; You shall not defraud; Honor your father and mother.'" He said to him, "Teacher, I have kept all these since my youth." Jesus, looking at him, loved him and said, "You lack one thing; go, sell what you own, and give the money to the poor, and you will have treasure in heaven; then come, follow me." When he heard this, he was shocked and went away grieving, for he had many possessions.

Then Jesus looked around and said to his disciples, "How hard it will be for those who have wealth to enter the kingdom of God!" And the disciples were perplexed at these words. But Jesus said to them again, "Children, how hard it is to enter the kingdom of God! It is easier for a camel to go through the eye of a needle than for someone who is rich to enter the kingdom of God." They were greatly astounded and said to one another,

"Then who can be saved?" Jesus looked at them and said, "For mortals it is impossible, but not for God; for God all things are possible."

Peter began to say to him, "Look, we have left everything and followed you." Jesus said, "Truly I tell you, there is no one who has left house or brothers or sisters or mother or father or children or fields, for my sake and for the sake of the good news, who will not receive a hundredfold now in this age— houses, brothers and sisters, mothers and children, and fields with persecutions—and in the age to come eternal life. But many who are first will be last, and the last will be first." (Mark 10:17-31)

One Sunday after worship I found a little book under the back row of sanctuary chairs, a toddler's book called *Pat the Bunny*. You may have seen this book filled with quiet projects for children to do during the service: button a button, open a door, pat some fur. This must have been the *New Revised Standard Version* for the last page was one I'd never seen before: the toddler could pull a lever and a paper dollar popped out of a slot in the cardboard cash machine. No doubt, the child had seen the real thing, watching as a grown-up put a card in a machine, punched in numbers, and grabbed the crisp new money. Toddlers surely will want one of those cards when they grow up.

In New York City it was once quite common for street people to station themselves near cash machines. It has become more rare since the mayor improved the quality of life in our city by getting homeless people off the streets, especially in tourist areas. (The quality of life for homeless people themselves was not considered a priority.) But street people are resilient and haven't completely disappeared. A man—it's usually a man, but occasionally a woman—opens the door of the bank: "Ma'am, I don't mean to disturb you, but if you have anything to share today I would be ever so grateful." On the way out, he opens the door again, saying, "God bless you. Have a good day"—whether or not he receives a donation. Now, it would be great if he had a sign with bold letters:

"IT IS EASIER FOR A CAMEL TO GO THROUGH THE EYE OF A NEEDLE THAN FOR SOMEONE WHO IS RICH TO ENTER THE KINGDOM OF HEAVEN."

No doubt such a sign will offend some people, but others might consider it creative and clever. With a wallet full of new twenties, they might slip a dollar or at least a quarter in the man's cup. If he could have a camel standing with him that would be even better—until a good church person comes along, someone who's been to a Bible study on Mark 10.

"That doesn't mean what you think," she says. "The Eye of the Needle was a small gate in the wall of Jerusalem about four feet high." The man reaches his hand high, trying to touch the camel's head. "Over seven feet, I'd say."

"Well, it would be very unlikely for a camel to go through the gate standing up," she answers. "How tall is your camel on its knees?" Just then the light turns green, the woman walks on and the man prays that no other church people will come by that day.

Most of us gave up the line about the little gate long ago (though we're still tempted by the possibility that the Greek word translated *camel* is very close to the word *cable*, and if you had a really large needle . . .). But we don't have to know Greek to get past the beggar's sign. This story can be summed up by saying, "Where your heart is there will your treasure be also." That's not exactly what Jesus said, but he used the same words. If none of this works, I can say to myself, "Where will Donald Trump and Bill Gates be when this text comes up in the lectionary?" You can fill in another name. Choose any name—as long as it's not mine.

Then I can go back to the cash machine in peace, as I did not long ago when I was downtown in Greenwich Village. I begin to punch in my Personal Identification Number and just then, someone taps me on the shoulder. I'm shocked because cash machine etiquette means you never get close enough to read someone's secret number and you surely don't get close enough to tap someone on the shoulder. I turn around to say, "Back off . . ."

It's Jesus, and he's got this camel.

He waits beside me while the machine whirrs. I withdraw $40 though I usually get $100. Then he turns to walk away, beckoning me to come along. It's New York City so no one seems to notice the camel. Or Jesus. A couple blocks down is Balducci's Market, an emporium of gourmet foods. Jesus stops in front of the windows, moving slowly from one to the other: huge silvery fish staring blankly from banks of ice, specialty cakes with fancy curls of icing, glistening bottles of virgin olive oil, strawberries and apricots dipped in chocolate. Just beyond the last window, a thin man has propped himself up against the market wall. He's sitting on a newspaper holding out a blue and white cup from the Greek diner. Jesus wants to know why the man is there. I tell him it's a very good spot since most people who go to Balducci's have plenty of money. But Jesus wants to know *why* he is there—why some people are buying hand-dipped strawberries while others are sitting outside the door. I tell him that it's all very complicated. The man may be mentally ill or he may be a drug addict or an alcoholic and giving him money will only make things worse, or he may be perfectly fine like a man I saw limping through the subway car asking for money, then later saw him running down the street—and I wish Jesus did not know I had $40 in my wallet. Then Jesus bends down and helps the man to his feet. "Go on into the store with her," Jesus says, nodding in my direction. "You must be pretty hungry. I'll take your place here for a while . . . "

Of course, I made it up—the part about Jesus and the camel. The part about Balducci's is true, and the thin man sitting on the sidewalk with the cup from the Greek diner. By now I'm sure the police have asked him to move on. I talked to him a few times and gave him a little money, but I never took him into Balducci's and I would never sell everything I own to give it to him.

How Do We Preach This Story We Do Not Want to Be In?

We won't try the little gate anymore, but the temptation to distance ourselves from this story remains. Over many years preaching on this text, I've discovered that the distance can come from an attentive, academically sound reading of the text:

This man was a fawning flatterer who wanted to add eternal life to his holdings. "Good Teacher," he began. Many commentators point out that his address was insincere and Jesus knew it.[1] This man was trying to flatter Jesus and expected Jesus to reciprocate—to say something like, "But I'm no better than you, my son. You seem to be a good man yourself." Not only did Jesus fail to return the compliment but he also refused to accept the designation for himself. "No one is good but God alone," Jesus said—causing decades of christological controversy later on. (Of course, Jesus had never read the Nicene Creed.) But what happens when we insist on seeing this man as an insincere flatterer? We can dismiss him. The problem isn't money—it's his attitude, his egocentric personality.

This man's theology was faulty. "What must I *do* to inherit eternal life?" he asked. "Nothing!" shout the Lutherans, who learned long ago that you don't have to *do* anything. But as far as we know, this man was not Lutheran. Still, it was a rather odd question. It sounds reasonable at first, but *do* and *inherit* clash, don't they? You inherit by virtue of birth: the farm, the crown, the estate, perhaps your father's pulpit (maybe some-day soon, your mother's pulpit). Usually, inheritance came from the good fortune of being the firstborn, though we know the prodigal son received a share even though he was the youngest. But inheriting is not something you *do*—it is something you *receive*. The man was asking the wrong question. Perhaps the Lutherans were right. It's not a story about money. It's a story about bad theology.

He got his wealth through dishonest means. You may have noticed long ago that Jesus' list of the commandments is odd. The first three are missing and the rest are out of order. Not only that, but Jesus has slipped in "You shall not defraud." (Matthew and Luke noticed and got rid of that line.) Ched Myers is not alone in seeing Jesus' addition as clear evidence that this man amassed his possessions through fraud—withholding wages, usurping property, neglecting widows and orphans.[2]

"Teacher," the man replied, "I have kept all these since my youth." He was a quick study—note that he didn't say "Good Teacher" this time. But surely we can't believe he kept all these commandments! (We've already decided he was an insincere flatterer!) Did he even notice that Jesus had added, "You shall not defraud"? Jesus didn't challenge the man's answer. But we will. This isn't a story about money—it's a story about *bad* money. It's about fraud.

The real issue is faith, not money. Jesus knew wealth was this man's problem, but for us it may be something else. Jesus seemed headed in that direction when he turned to the disciples to make sure they understood what just happened. "How hard it will be for those who have wealth to enter the kingdom of God!" Jesus said. And the disciples were perplexed—as was often the case. Then Jesus addressed them more intimately, saying, "Children, how hard it is to enter the kingdom of God!"

"Amen!" we shout. "The road is wide but the gate is narrow . . . Many are called but few are chosen. Many will call out, 'Lord, Lord' . . ." etc. Shouldn't Jesus have said, "How hard it is *for the rich* to enter the kingdom of God"? But Jesus didn't say that. Jesus said, "Children, how hard it is to enter the kingdom of God!" Did the disciples finally understand the preceding story about receiving the kingdom of God as a little child? This story isn't really about money; it's about becoming children of God.

Just then, Jesus taps us on the shoulder, and he's got this camel. I didn't let Jesus finish what he was saying: "It is easier for a camel to go through the eye of a needle than for someone who is rich to enter the kingdom of God." Hearing this, the disciples were greatly astounded and said to one another, "Then who can be saved?" Whatever else "apostolic succession" means, it means we stand in a long line of those who do not want to hear about money!

"When the man heard Jesus' words he went away grieving, for he had many possessions." But Jesus loved this man. The text says it plainly: "Jesus, looking at him, loved him." This is the only time in Mark's gospel where we are told that Jesus loved someone.[3] Did this man love Jesus? Or as Jesus would ask, "Did this man love God who alone is good"? It is not a simple question, as W. H. Auden reminds us at the end of his poem about love:

Will it come like a change in the weather?
   Will its greeting be courteous or rough?
Will it alter my life all together?
   Oh, tell me the truth about love.[4]

Perhaps that's what he was most afraid of—that loving God would alter his life altogether, so he walked away grieving. It may be what we're most afraid of, so we walk away, too.

In spite of all the arguments, this is a text about money. How does this text mark our time? And how does our time mark this text? We're not even sure what time it is. Is it the time marked by 22 million new jobs or by 43 million Americans without health insurance (not to mention the rest of the world)? Is it measured in the new luxury high-rise apartments on Manhattan's Upper West Side or by the people in neon orange vests picking up trash in Riverside Park on their way from welfare to "meaningful work"?

The promise of wealth is not new but has long fueled the American dream. In 1835 Alexis de Tocqueville observed that our passion for wealth seemed built into democracy itself:

> When the reverence which belonged to what is old has vanished, birth, condition, and profession no longer distinguish men . . . hardly anything but money remains to create strongly marked differences between them, and to raise some of them above the common level. The distinction originating in wealth is increased by the disappearance or diminution of all other distinctions.[5]

We can't be kings or queens, but we can rise above the masses by amassing! This may have been true for a long time, but what has shifted in the last few years is the instant, extravagant wealth of young Internet wizards and the incredible riches reaped by some in the stock market. At the height of the technology boom, high school students in Palo Alto, California, offered a glimpse of what the expectation of wealth is like. Alexis T., age seventeen: "In school you're learning as fast as you can so you can apply it as fast as you can so that you can become rich and successful by age

24, because that's what happens here." A classmate named Lisa shared her feelings of being left behind: "My parents are doctors . . . but when they see tons of money, I think they feel sort of left out. Compared to the C.E.O. of Cisco Systems, my dad feels totally insignificant."[6] The September 18, 2000, issue of *Barron's* business magazine reported that in the past five years the number of millionaires had doubled from 3.4 million to 7.2 million.[7] Doubled, in five years, and still growing.

This time is different even from the era of the Rockefellers, Vanderbilts, and Morgans. J. P. Morgan believed that no executive should make "more than twenty times the pay of the lowest worker . . ."[8] "But that quaint idea has been set aside," says Graef Crystal in his book *In Search of Excess*. "In 1999 the frequently cited figure is that CEO compensation is 419 times that of the average line worker."[9] No doubt that figure will be even more outrageous by the time you are reading these words.

Such wealth is rare, but stories like these set a tone of unlimited wealth and spending, the "trickle-down" theory of possessions and greed. Those who will never see such staggering profits begin to measure their lives by the excesses of those at the top. Sociologist Barrie Thorne defines a *working family* as "middle-class people trying to live only on wages, not earnings from investments . . . They can't do it," he says, "and they feel non-affluent and not adequately compensated for the number of hours they must work to make ends meet."[10]

The problem is not just one man who had many possessions but a whole system that creates wealth for a few at the expense of the common good. In her book *Chaos or Community*, Holly Sklar presents stories and statistics tracing the tragic gap between rich and poor.

- "The United States is the poorest richest country in the world . . . it lags behind other industrialized democracies in assuring basic human needs—health care being today's best known example."[11]
- "If the U.S. government were a parent, it would be guilty of child abuse." Mortality rates for black babies in the U.S. are

intolerable; our country ranks way down the list behind such nations as Jamaica, Sri Lanka, Poland, Cuba, and Kuwait.[12]

Sklar summarizes the graphs and statistics, saying, "We have a greed surplus and a justice deficit."[13]

John Cobb and Herman Daly's book, *For the Common Good,* argues that the GNP is inadequate as a measure of economic well-being. Referring to their work, James Childs writes: "Increase in the GNP does not necessarily mean increase in economic welfare. That is, simple growth is not always simply good."[14]

Does the church have anything to say about this excessive greed? In a *New York Times* editorial, British writer Geoffrey Wheatcroft marvels at the role played by religion in the U.S. political campaign. Citing statements made by presidential and vice-presidential candidates in the 2000 campaign, Wheatcroft ends with Al Gore's question, "What would Jesus do?"

"What indeed?" asks Wheatcroft. "What would Jesus do about the budget surplus, China trade or Sierra Leone? *The gospels provide remarkably little guidance about practical conduct, certainly not in military or economic matters*"[15] (italics added).

Is Wheatcroft right—do the Gospels provide remarkably little guidance in economic matters? It's true that the Bible doesn't weigh in on "the budget surplus or China trade." Scripture says nothing about the WTO or the IMF, GATT, or NAFTA (the Bible seldom speaks in initials!). But there's a deep river running through the Bible that speaks clearly against the disparity between rich and poor. Some might affirm the accumulation of wealth by citing Deuteronomy 28 where wealth seems a sign of God's favor and poverty a sign of God's curse. But the Hebrew prophets Amos, Isaiah, and Jeremiah soundly critiqued this theology of wealth. Jesus stood the theology of wealth on its head when he told the parable of the rich man and Lazarus. Jesus' painful picture of Lazarus seems deliberately drawn to correspond to pictures in Deuteronomy 28 where the cursed poor are covered with sores from head to foot.[16] That is, the ones cursed looked just like Lazarus. But in Jesus' story it is Lazarus who is carried to the bosom of Abraham and the rich man who is cursed in the eternal fire.

And then, there's that camel.

It does little good to hang the Ten Commandments on the courthouse wall if we say nothing about possessions and greed. Remember? The rich man had observed the commandments since his youth. Or maybe the commandments are only supposed to restore sexual morality throughout the land, or at least, in the White House. But do we have anything to say about possessions, about wealth and greed? Walter Brueggemann does offer a word:

> As we Americans grow wealthier and wealthier, money is becoming a kind of narcotic for us. We hardly notice our own prosperity or the poverty of so many others . . .
>
> Consumerism is not simply a marketing strategy. It has become a demonic spiritual force among us, and the theological question facing us is whether the gospel has the power to help us withstand it.[17]

It is unlikely that Brueggemann will ever run for public office. He challenges the claim that the gospel has nothing to say about economic matters and isn't afraid to use theological language to name consumerism a "demonic spiritual force." But what will people do with this strong word, with accurate economic analysis and strong theological critique? Holly Sklar is right: "We have a greed surplus and a justice deficit." Cobb and Daly are also right: "Simple growth is not simply good." Brueggemann, too: "Consumerism is a demonic spiritual force among us." People listening to the sermon may reach for a pen, jotting these phrases on the back of the bulletin. "Something has to be done about this!" Months later they pull the crumpled bulletin out of their suit coat pocket or purse and toss it in the wastebasket, defeated and guilty for they haven't done a thing. The systemic evils of corporate greed and consuming materialism can cause people to walk away not so much grieving as completely overwhelmed.

This story *is* bigger and more complicated than one rich man. We can see a wealthy nation-under-God kneeling before Jesus or a wealthy denomination closing down another poor urban congregation. *But there's also a camel in the sanctuary*—and the camel doesn't show up only for Stewardship Month. Jesus didn't say, "Go, sell what you own and increase your pledge." He said, "Give to the poor." In the overall scheme of Mark's gospel, the poor widow in chapter 12 stands as the counterpoint to the rich man. The rich man fleshes out Jesus' picture of the word sown among thorns: "these are the ones who hear the word, ['Teacher, I have observed all these commandments since my youth!'] but the cares of the world, and the lure of wealth, and the desire for other things come in and choke the word, and it yields nothing" (Mark 4:18-19). It's the poor widow who is good soil in a gospel where there's little good soil to be found.[18]

But we do not want to be the poor widow any more than we want to admit that we're the rich man!

"Then who can be saved?" we ask. "For mortals it is impossible, but not for God; for God all things are possible." Jesus' words sound trite, almost formulaic. We can imagine Jesus' words on one of those motivational posters in the corporate conference room. You've seen them, haven't you? A dramatic color photograph of a lone mountain climber reaching the summit: "With God all things are possible." But Jesus wasn't thinking about such a poster. Jesus draws us back to words spoken at the edge of the river:

> Surely, this commandment that I am commanding you today is not too hard for you, nor is it too far away. It is not in heaven, that you should say, "Who will go up to heaven for us, and get it for us so that we may hear it and observe it?" Neither is it beyond the sea, that you should say, "Who will cross to the other side of the sea for us, and get it for us so that we may hear it and observe it?" No, the word is very near to you; it is in your mouth and in your heart for you to observe. (Deuteronomy 30:11-14)

That is, this word about wealth is not only about a system high as the sky or wide as the sea. This word is in your mouth and heart for you to do. "Go, sell what you own, and give to the poor, and you will have treasure in heaven; then, come, follow me." For years, I've tried to convince Jesus that his verbs are in the wrong order—he *should* have said, "Come, follow me," and I will empower you to "go, sell, and give to the poor." Dietrich Bonhoeffer insists that all these verbs be held together. He focuses on Matthew's version of the story in *The Cost of Discipleship*. For Bonhoeffer, this story goes to the heart of his teaching about cheap grace: "Only those who obey can believe, and only those who believe can obey."[19]

Of course, such a paradox can itself be a form of avoidance! But Bonhoeffer was not one to fall into the arms of a paradox when all else fails—neither does he commend such falling to us. We now think of Bonhoeffer on a global stage, but his writing was very local, from a pastor's heart. He imagines a pastoral conversation with a man who says, "I have lost the faith I once had." The pastor and the man talk back and forth but get nowhere until the pastor is at a loss about what to say next. "Why?" Bonhoeffer asks. "Because the pastor only remembers the first half of the proposition, 'Only those who believe obey.'"

But this does not help, for faith is just what this particular man finds impossible. "So the pastor throws up the sponge," Bonhoeffer says, "and leaves the poor man to his fate. And yet this ought to be the turning-point . . . It is now time to take the bull by the horns, and say: 'Only those who obey believe' . . . In the name of Christ, [the pastor] must exhort the man to obedience, to action, to take the first step. He must say: 'Tear yourself away from all other attachments, and follow [Christ].'"[20]

But it is not easy to take the bull by the horns whether in pastoral counseling or preaching. On Sunday morning, one person sits listening alongside others in the sanctuary. He or she is part of a global economic system; part of the holy, catholic, and apostolic church; part of this congregation, but often utterly alone in dealing with money and possessions. Sharon Daloz Parks acknowledges this sense of isolation: "In the domain of economic life, we typically remain strangers to one another—each of us essentially alone with our sense of busyness and cumber, fear and guilt."[21] Her words are part of the chapter "Household Economics" in the down-to-earth book *Practicing Our Faith*. The book's title plays on the word *practicing,* a reminder that living our faith does not come naturally. It takes *practice*—like shooting free throws or repeating scales on the piano. Religious communities such as the Quakers and the Mennonites have long known something crucial: "as lone individuals, it is very difficult to change our economic patterns."[22] Is it possible to imagine following the example of a Mennonite congregation in the Midwest?

> [The congregation] requires . . . that everyone belong to a small group . . . that meets regularly . . . At least once a year, within their small group, they discuss their individual and collective practice of household economics. This typically involves reflecting together on how much income they have and how they earn, invest, and spend it. One group began this discussion by sharing their 1040 tax forms with each other.[23]

That's one way to take the bull by the horns—and some pastors may imagine such a recommendation to be their last before moving on to another parish! But we can't break free from the grip of possessions by ourselves. Jesus' last words to the rich man were, "Come, follow me." Jesus' promise to the disciples was a new community: "in this age—houses, brothers and sisters, mothers and children, and fields with persecutions—and in the age to come eternal life." Jesus had redefined this new family at the end of chapter 3; persecutions were becoming a reality by the time Mark wrote this story down. Proposing simplicity in an age that thrives on spending may not get us killed, but it could well mark us as unrealistic and more than a little naïve.

We're up against these twin temptations when preaching this text:

- "It's not really about money; let's talk about faith," or
- "It is about money; let's talk about dismantling the global economic system of exploitative, greed-centered capitalism."

But both of these can distance us from Mark's story of Jesus and the rich man. How can we help people enter this story? How can we be serious about Jesus' call to obedience?

- **Honor the inadequate and the imperfect—and keep pressing on.**
  When the Industrial Areas Foundation (IAF) started organizing in Brooklyn for what eventually became Nehemiah housing for the working poor, their first goal was a traffic light at a dangerous intersection. They knew this light wouldn't overturn the tragic inequities that plagued Bedford-Stuyvesant, but it was a beginning. As pastors we can stand with people as they try small steps.

- **Provide spaces for talking about household economics.**
  I have come to have deep respect for the wisdom of ordinary women and men in congregations. There are parents who can help other parents as they fight an uphill battle against the materialism that is consuming children at an early age. There are people who struggle with downsizing, layoffs, pension funds, and socially responsible investments. Give people a chance to share this wisdom with one another.

- **Invite people into the conversation when we preach about wealth.**
  Talk to people in their workplace. Put a question box at the back of the sanctuary or a tear-off insert in the bulletin. If you're in a congregation that's "wired," invite e-mail responses to a question like: "How would my life change if my salary were cut in half next year?" or "If you were the rich man in this story how would you argue with what Jesus told you to do?" The sermon can also be an invitation for further conversation: a discussion immediately after worship, an educational forum the next Sunday, a series on wealth and poverty, etc.

- **Form respectful, reciprocal partnerships across class lines.**
  Congregations have been reaching across economic divides for some time. Early on these partnerships were often very one-sided: clothes, money, and food from the wealthy to the poor. But now many have moved beyond this one-way street and transformation is happening in poor and rich congregations alike.

- **Stand with the people, not over against them.**
  Some Sunday put several things at the front of the sanctuary: laptop computer, VCR, TV, car keys, tennis racket, and mountain bike. "These are some of the things I own. What do you think I could do without?"
- **Tell the truth that seldom gets a hearing.**
  With TV and radio stations, Internet, and newspapers now owned by a few major corporations, it can be hard to hear the truth that nobody wants to tell. Scour the papers for stories that are buried on page 14, stories about the increase in lines at the soup kitchen or food pantry, stories about CEO wages, stories about United States aid to developing countries. Enlist volunteers to help with this detective work—clipping articles, reading newspapers from other countries on the Internet, and even checking the CIA Web site. The site analyzes countries around the globe in terms of demographics, economic strength, military installations, etc. In their analysis of the United States, they note that a major security problem is the income disparity gap.

Pastors and parishioners can also think together about how Jesus' call to obedience shapes our communal life as a congregation. Some congregations are themselves important players on big stages, with community development corporations, housing projects, job training programs, and charter schools. They are forces to be reckoned with in city politics. But small congregations also make decisions about land and buildings, budgets and debts.

Some time ago, I talked with a friend who is pastor in a New England city. "How's your renovation going?" I asked her. "It's almost finished," she said, "but we ran out of money for the sanctuary." (What could be more important than the worship space? I wondered to myself.) The congregation renovated the church basement used as a shelter for homeless people—made it more hospitable, put in two sets of showers, improved the kitchen. On the Sunday before the shelter opened, worship began in the sanctuary as usual. Just before Communion, the congregation processed down to the shelter carrying the bread and the cup.

Then they shared Communion around the empty beds in the renovated space. "The body of Christ given for you." By evening
the shelter beds were filled and the sanctuary still needed a lot
of work.[24]

Will we dare to let this text mark our time? It is not easy to
preach this story we do not want to be in. I have no doubt that
someone will teach our children about cash machines. But you
and I are called to tell them about Jesus—and the camel.

I hope we won't forget.

CHAPTER FOUR

Water on a Desert Road: Splashing in the Scroll of Isaiah

Then an angel of the Lord said to Philip, "Get up and go toward the south to the road that goes down from Jerusalem to Gaza." (This is a wilderness road.) So he got up and went. Now there was an Ethiopian eunuch, a court official of the Candace, queen of the Ethiopians, in charge of her entire treasury. He had come to Jerusalem to worship and was returning home; seated in his chariot, he was reading the prophet Isaiah. Then the Spirit said to Philip, "Go over to this chariot and join it." So Philip ran up to it and heard him reading the prophet Isaiah. He asked, "Do you understand what you are reading?" He replied, "How can I, unless someone guides me?" And he invited Philip to get in and sit beside him. Now the passage of the scripture that he was reading was this:
"Like a sheep he was led to the slaughter,
    and like a lamb silent before its shearer,
        so he does not open his mouth.
In his humiliation justice was denied him.
    Who can describe his generation?
        For his life is taken away from the earth."
The eunuch asked Philip, "About whom, may I ask you, does

the prophet say this, about himself or about someone else?" Then Philip began to speak, and starting with this scripture, he proclaimed to him the good news about Jesus. As they were going along the road, they came to some water; and the eunuch said, "Look, here is water! What is to prevent me from being baptized?" He commanded the chariot to stop, and both of them, Philip and the eunuch, went down into the water, and Philip baptized him. When they came up out of the water, the Spirit of the Lord snatched Philip away; the eunuch saw him no more, and went on his way rejoicing. But Philip found himself at Azotus, and as he was passing through the region, he proclaimed the good news to all the towns until he came to Caesarea. (Acts 8:26-40)

It had not occurred to Philip to go south on the road from Jerusalem to Gaza. Philip had just completed a successful mission in Samaria. Response to his preaching was the envy of every preacher for "the crowds with one accord listened eagerly" to what he had to say. Many women and men were baptized, including Simon, the powerful magician. Then suddenly Philip disappeared from view (Acts 8:4-13).

"Now when the apostles in Jerusalem heard that Samaria had accepted the word of God, they sent Peter and John to them." They had specific reasons for going—to pray that the Samaritans "might receive the Holy Spirit (for as yet the Spirit had not come upon any of them; they had only been baptized in the name of the Lord Jesus)" (Acts 8:14-16). That is, there were questions about the efficacy of Philip's ministry. Back in chapter 6, Philip had been appointed a deacon, called specifically to care for those neglected in the daily distribution so the apostles weren't distracted from preaching. Then why was Philip preaching and baptizing? Was he a free agent whose evangelistic efforts have to be verified by the Jerusalem authorities?

Such questions remain beneath the surface when, suddenly, Philip reappeared. It is clear that God had other plans for Philip: "Then an angel of the Lord said to Philip, 'Get up and go toward the south to the road that goes down from Jerusalem to Gaza' (This is a wilderness road)" (Acts 8:26). That last sentence was not part of the angel's speech. It is the storyteller's aside to the audience: "This is *erene*: a desert road." It passes by almost without notice as the narrator goes on—"So he got up and went," even though it was not his idea.

"Now [on that same road] there was an Ethiopian, a eunuch, a court official of the Candace, queen of the Ethiopians, in charge of her entire treasury" (Acts 8:27).

The narrator slows us down with particularities—even more pronounced in Greek than in English: a man / an Ethiopian / a eunuch / an official of Candace / queen of the Ethiopians / who was over all of her treasury. Slow down. You almost missed the desert road!

The man was an Ethiopian. To Homer, Ethiopia was the farthest limit of humankind, the land where the sun set. Most likely, the term refers to the kingdom of Nubia, called Cush in the Old Testament. This was the nation south of Egypt, along the Nile[1]— an African nation, not on most maps in the back of the Bible. The man in the chariot was a black-skinned African. He does not fit the adjectives used to describe Africans in eighteenth-century tracts supporting slavery.[2] He was not "ignorant" or "uneducated" (he was reading aloud, most likely in Greek); he was not "idle" or "brutish" (he was a court official with a position of high rank); and he surely was not "treacherous or thievish" (he was in charge of all the queen's treasury—the Alan Greenspan of Ethiopia!). Luke and his readers would have seen this Ethiopian in a far different light than later generations of Europeans and Americans. Luke's decision to identify the man on the road as an Ethiopian cannot be accidental. The Ethiopian's baptism fulfilled Jesus' promise, for the gospel had now reached the place where the sun sets—"the ends of the earth" (Acts 1:8).

But this poses a problem: tradition had named Cornelius as the first Gentile convert. The Ethiopian could not be allowed to preempt Cornelius! Was this because Cornelius was white? Was the Ethiopian's baptism invalid—after all, questions had already been raised about Philip's baptisms in Samaria? Was the Ethiopian an authentic Gentile? Had the Ethiopian been adequately catechized? The Ethiopian's profession of faith, "I believe that Jesus

Christ is the Son of God," has been relegated to the footnotes, though it was cited by many of the church fathers before the Constantinian era.[3] Why all these questions? Was this an attempt to discount Philip, the Ethiopian, or both?

Or was it the fact that this man was not only an Ethiopian, he was also a eunuch? Luke repeats *eunoukos* five times in this story. We are not allowed to forget that the man in the chariot is a eunuch. (Though he doesn't repeat the word *Ethiopian* that doesn't mean we should forget that either.) This eunuch is an Ethiopian and remains an Ethiopian—though some of the church fathers claimed he was made white when he was baptized![4]

The man was a eunuch. But what is a eunuch? We seldom speak of eunuchs—and when we do, some are likely to cross their legs! Even as we cannot make the Ethiopian simply a *foreigner*, we cannot claim that εὐνοῦχος means simply an *official* as some have translated this verse. Hans Conzelmann argues for maintaining the word *eunuch* by pointing to the Greek text where the two words appear side by side: ". . . εὐνοῦχος 'eunuch,' as used here does not refer to a position (that would be δυνάστης), but to one who has been castrated."[5] The term δυνάστης would be redundant if εὐνοῦχος means "official." That is, the text would then read, "He was an official official!" Hard as it is for us to talk about eunuchs, the Ethiopian man was one.

Luke presupposes that readers have a particular knowledge of eunuchs. I am indebted to New Testament scholar Cottrel Rick Carson for his in-depth study of eunuchs.[6] His reading of primary sources on eunuchs ranges widely among classical Greek and Latin texts, as well as the Septuagint. Two kinds of eunuchs are described in classical texts: those castrated from birth and those castrated after reaching physical manhood.[7] Both ended up alienated from their birth families, making loyalty to the monarch a matter of life and death. Eunuchs were involved in three primary tasks: 1) personal domestic service, often tutoring royal children; 2) the military—what could be better, they could never covet hereditary power; and 3) positions in the bureaucracy.[8]

Eunuchs (*sarisim* in Hebrew) are mentioned fifty-six times in the Septuagint, serving in all three of these capacities. In

Jeremiah 38:7 we read: "Ebed-melech the Ethiopian, a eunuch in the king's house, heard that they had put Jeremiah into the cistern." The Ethiopian eunuch went to speak to the king to report this wickedness and the king appointed Ebed-melech to take some men to pull Jeremiah from the well. Did Luke find the Ethiopian eunuch in the book of Jeremiah? Some of his readers might have wondered.[9]

But the biblical texts tell us nothing about the physical appearance of eunuchs, perhaps because earlier readers would have known this. However, it is not well known among us:

- A eunuch's body took on certain aspects regarded as "feminine."
- A eunuch's skin was uniquely wrinkled, even at an early age.
- A eunuch's pubic hair grew in feminine rather than masculine patterns.

These physical characteristics are even more pronounced for those who are eunuchs from birth:

- Their hairlines were those of teenagers: "The eunuch is considered, in part, a boy—no matter what his age."[10]
- Eunuchs had "immature" genitalia, but this did not mean they were asexual.
- The eunuch's voice was that of a teenager—like *castrati*, the boy sopranos who sang for years in church choirs before such castrations were condemned.
- Eunuchs appeared "gangly or awkward" due to irregular growth of the bones in their arms and legs; "osteoporosis, curvature of the spine, and joint deformities" were common by middle age.[11]

Luke's readers would thus have seen a dissonant image—like a double-exposed photograph:

An Ethiopian—usually portrayed in classical texts and the Septuagint as muscular, tall, dark, with strongly defined features.[12]

A eunuch—probably middle aged to be in such a prominent position, perhaps deformed by the misshapen fitting of his limbs.

We take this double-exposed photograph with us as the story moves on. Once more God intervened: "Then the Spirit said to Philip, 'Go over to this chariot and join it.' So Philip ran up to it and heard him reading the prophet Isaiah. He asked, 'Do you understand what you are reading?' He replied, 'How can I unless someone guides me?'" So he invited Philip to get in and sit beside him. The eunuch was reading aloud as was the custom in antiquity. Had he been reading since he left Jerusalem? Luke quotes Isaiah 53, verses 7 and 8. But isn't it likely that the Ethiopian eunuch had begun with the first verses of this chapter?

> Who has believed what we have heard?
> And to whom has the arm of the LORD been revealed?
> For he grew up before him like a young plant,
>   and like a root out of dry ground;
> he had no form or majesty that we should look at him,
>   nothing in his appearance that we should desire him.
>
> (Isaiah 53:1-2)

What would the eunuch have heard if he read those words on his way from Jerusalem?

Like a root out of dry ground—a dry tree they sometimes called him, behind his back or even to his face . . . a dry tree on a desert road.

He had no form or majesty that we should look at him, nothing in his appearance that we should desire him—gangly, effeminate, wrinkled, too boyish for a grown man, misshapen.

And what about the verses he was reading when Philip came running up? Had he been humiliated because of being a eunuch, even though he was an important official? Had justice been denied him? He had traveled a long way to worship in Jerusalem, but how could he have been allowed into the assembly of the Lord? He must have known the holiness code: "No one whose testicles are crushed or whose penis is cut off shall be admitted to the assembly of the LORD" (Deuteronomy 23:1). It was written down. He was an educated man; he could read the words for himself.

"About whom, may I ask you, does the prophet say this, about himself or about someone else?" Or about me, he might have wondered. Does the prophet look like me? Am I in this text?

"Then Philip began to speak . . ."

Wait, Philip, wait. Have we allowed the eunuch's question to mark time with us? It's a very good question: "About whom, may I ask you, does the prophet say this, about himself or about someone else?" Isaiah never answered that question. It's almost impossible for us as Christians to let the eunuch's question hang in the air for long—because we *know* the answer. We know of whom Isaiah speaks for these verses make up "The Fourth Servant Song." But that was not Isaiah's designation.

To the eunuch riding in his chariot, Isaiah's words could have meant someone like him.

To Jewish people, this unnamed one, not called a "servant" here, is almost always the people Israel. On Yom Kippur, people in Reform Jewish congregations join in a responsive reading from *Gates of Repentance: The New Union Prayer Book for the Days of Awe*. The reading ends with the remembrance of martyrs of many nations and lands,[13] but the central portion remembers the Jewish martyrs throughout history with these words:

> They had no outward grace to attract the eye, no beauty to win the heart.
> *They were despised and rejected, a people of pains and acquainted with grief.*
> . . . .
> Like lambs led to the slaughter, like sheep standing dumb before their shearers, they never uttered a cry.
> *By violence and injustice were they carried off.*
> Who cared about their fate, when they were cut off from the land of the living? [14]

"About whom, may I ask you, does the prophet say this, about himself or about someone else? Then Philip began to speak, and starting with this scripture, he proclaimed to him the good news about Jesus." *But Jesus was not in the text.* Christians affirm

Philip's answer for he had taken up the interpretive work modeled by Jesus at the end of Luke. As two disciples stood still, looking sad on the Emmaus road, Jesus (the stranger) spoke to them about Messiah " . . . beginning with Moses and all the prophets, he interpreted to them the things about himself in all the scriptures" (Luke 24:27).

Now Philip was continuing that work. Jesus had said it would be so at the beginning of Acts: "But you will receive power when the Holy Spirit has come upon you; and you will be my witnesses in Jerusalem, in all Judea and Samaria, and to the ends of the earth" (Acts 1:8). As Christians we believe that the Spirit who told Philip to join that chariot revealed Jesus where the name was not written. Or—to frame it differently—Isaiah's words had authentic meaning within Isaiah's time, but when Jesus' followers tried to make sense of his tragic death they "saw" Jesus in Isaiah's servant. However we frame it, one thing is clear: Without a witness *beyond the written text* Philip could not have seen Jesus *in the text.*

How far did they ride that day on the desert road? Did they keep unrolling the scroll from chapter 53 to chapter 56?

> Do not let the foreigner joined to the LORD say,
>   "The LORD will surely separate me from his people";
> and do not let the eunuch say,
>   "I am just a dry tree."
> For thus says the LORD:
> To eunuchs who keep my sabbaths,
>   who choose the things that please me
>   and hold fast my covenant,
> I will give, in my house and within my walls,
>   a monument and a name
>   better than sons and daughters;
> I will give an everlasting name
>   that shall not be cut off. (Isaiah 56:3-5)

Could it be—"a monument and a name better than sons and daughters" for the childless eunuch? A place in God's house for the one excluded from "the assembly of the LORD"? How could Isaiah say this? *The prohibition was written down.* Where did this prophet whom we call "Third Isaiah" get this new word? "The Spirit of the Lord GOD is upon me," wrote the prophet, "because the LORD has anointed me . . . he has sent me to bring good news to the oppressed . . ." (Isaiah 61:1a). The Spirit did not wait for Jesus to read these verses in Nazareth. In the Spirit's power Isaiah dared to proclaim a new word, different from what was written down. If he had been a strict literalist, he could not have spoken this new word.

Of course we have no idea how far Philip and the Ethiopian eunuch rode together that day or how far they read in the scroll of Isaiah. But we can be quite certain that Luke had read that far! Robert Tannehill is not alone in hearing Isaiah's prophecy behind this story:

> This passage may well stand in the background of our scene, for Isa. 56:3-8 is concerned with two excluded classes: the eunuch and the foreigner. The Ethiopian eunuch is both. The narrator's acquaintance with this passage is suggested by the fact that it comes from the section of Scripture most heavily used in Luke-Acts (Isaiah 40–66).[15]

What Isaiah promised in the future becomes present tense on the desert road. It is intriguing to note that when Isaiah 56 is appointed as a lectionary reading, the verses about eunuchs are excluded. Only the promise to foreigners is read and the eunuch is hidden in the comma (Isaiah 56:1, 6-8). No doubt this can be explained by the decision to pair the Isaiah text with the Gospel reading that is the story of Jesus and the Canaanite woman, a foreigner who claims her right to the crumbs from the master's table (Matthew 15:21-28; Proper 15, Year A, in the *Revised Common Lectionary*). The Acts story itself is read on one of the Sundays after Easter when there is no reading from Hebrew scripture. Thus, people in congregations never hear Isaiah 56 and Acts 8 together.

How is the story of the Ethiopian eunuch unfolding among us? How does this text mark time with us? How does our time mark the text? We come to this story with our own particularities. In recent years, this story has drawn the attention of several

African-American New Testament scholars.[16] They have opened our eyes to the African identity of this man, to the color of his skin, to his high level of education and his position of power. Don't forget: the man in the chariot was an Ethiopian, not a generic "foreigner."

But he was also a eunuch. There was a particular sexual dimension to this man that has made him very compelling to gay, lesbian, bisexual, and transgender people. Here I want to be very clear: Luke was not writing about a homosexual. That term would have been as indecipherable to Luke as "eunuch" is for most of us.[17] But there are analogies. We recall Michael Fishbane's question, "To what does this matter compare?" What hermeneutical space is opened up when we consider possible "similitudes" to the eunuch in this time of history?[18]

- The eunuch is a man, yet he does not measure up to the culture's definition of what is masculine.
- The eunuch is defined by his genitals even if the term *eunuch* is sometimes used metaphorically. This seems to be the case when Jesus refers to eunuchs in Matthew. Responding to the disciples' difficulty with his words forbidding divorce and remarriage, Jesus says, "Not everyone can accept this teaching, but only those to whom it is given. For there are eunuchs who have been so from birth, and there are eunuchs who have been made eunuchs by others, and there are eunuchs who have made themselves eunuchs for the sake of the kingdom of heaven. Let anyone accept this who can" (Matthew 19:11-12). Because of the context, it is commonly assumed that Jesus was referring to celibacy rather than physical castration.
- The eunuch often holds positions of responsibility in the military, as a teacher, as a personal attendant to kings and queens, as a financial officer—but he is still seen as "other" in the culture.[19]
- Even if he attains high positions in the military or the bureaucracy, the holiness code makes it clear that a eunuch has no place "in the assembly of the LORD."

The eunuch was defined by sex whether or not he was sexually active. Indeed, sexual promiscuity was a favorite charge against eunuchs, as Carson discovered in reading several ancient texts. In 399 CE a eunuch named Eutropius became consul of the Eastern Empire, the first and only eunuch to hold this position. This did not sit well with Claudian, the state poet, so he wrote a long poem to undermine the character of the powerful eunuch. Jacqueline Long tells the story in her book *Claudian's In Eutropium: Or How, When, and Why to Slander a Eunuch:*

> Claudian's indictment is that sex was the only thing Eutropius had to offer. He has no other skill or strength with which he might serve. His many resales constitute the testimony of his masters that they found him worthless.[20]

But surely sex was not the only thing Eutropius had to offer or it is unlikely he would have attained such a prominent position. No doubt, it was his very prominence that brought on the attack. Eunuchs were accepted and often honored as long as they didn't go beyond what was considered their proper status.

Similar charges are made against gay men and lesbians—"Sex is the only thing you people think about!" or, "It's okay if you're gay, just don't flaunt it!" (That is, do not come to church with your partner and do not assume that the two of you can be photographed together for the church directory.) We need not turn the eunuch into a homosexual to see the *similitude* between his life and the lives of those judged as "other" based on sexuality alone. Though there have been significant changes in many fields, this "sexual otherness" is still the definitive word in the church.

If there is any issue that marks this time in the church's life, it is the ongoing debate about homosexuality. Many wish the whole subject would go away. Some say this issue is purposely diverting the church's attention from dealing with the story of the rich man—we're so busy talking about sex that we don't have time to talk about wealth and poverty. I often wish this debate would go away. But then I remember the words of our departed sister Audre

Lorde: "Sometimes we are blessed with being able to choose the time and the arena and the manner of our revolution, but more usually we must do battle wherever we are standing."[21] This is where we are standing. This issue marks our time in urgent ways.

Acts 8 and Isaiah 56 provide models for working with biblical texts that can be far more helpful than ongoing debates over verses in Leviticus, Romans, and Corinthians. *We have reached an exegetical impasse.* How many times can we exegete Paul's use of the terms *malakoi* and *arsenokoitai*?[22] By now most people have heard the long list of laws we've set aside in the holiness codes: eating shellfish and wearing two kinds of cloth—or if you're in a rural area, breeding two different kinds of cattle (my own father bred Holsteins with Guernseys!). But sexuality is not the same as eating shellfish. Some cling to the literal words of texts about sex with a tenacity unknown for texts about wealth and poverty. Some support a more affirmative position by boiling all scripture down to the Great Commandments—love God with all your being and love your neighbor as yourself. Others trust the transforming power of human experience: people in our families and circles of friends got divorced. Good people, faithful people get divorced and remarry, including ministers and bishops. Church policy changed, though Jesus' words against divorce and remarriage remain abundantly clear in Greek and in English.[23] Many have decided to leave the Bible behind all together, trusting wisdom from other disciplines to change people's minds. Homosexuality will someday seem as natural as the earth revolving around the sun. (All we need is a Copernican revolution in human sexuality.)

But the Bible remains the book of the church, the norm for its faith and life. It is the space in which we stand together—even though we interpret the words in radically different ways. The Bible cannot be summarized in the Golden Rule or the Great Commandment nor can it be reduced to a rulebook of our favorite proof texts. Many faithful Christians are confused, torn between what they recognize as *selective* literalism[24] and teachings that seem to abandon the Bible all together. We have not yet plumbed the depths of the Bible's wisdom nor have we given sufficient attention to how the Bible itself works with texts. The Spirit draws us back to the desert road, back to the scroll that had to be *interpreted* not because the Ethiopian eunuch was ignorant but because the words in the scroll couldn't answer his question: "About whom does the prophet say this?" Philip couldn't rely only on the words written down. He "saw" Jesus even though the name wasn't in Isaiah's text. But this is not a matter of the "new" testament overcoming the "old"—Jesus' love replacing Mosaic law, or Jesus' compassion trumping the purity codes. Isaiah had already moved beyond the words written down. His vision of a new community out of exile depended on the Spirit's anointing. Krister Stendahl, New Testament scholar and Bishop Emeritus of Stockholm, urges us to remember, "the church and the scriptures live by interpretation, not by repristination. Faithful interpretation is faithfilled creativity."[25]

Isaiah interpreted the words of tradition in a new way on this side of the exile. Isaiah 56 has taken on special meaning for many gay and lesbian people. An Orthodox rabbi, who is gay, wrote an essay for the journal *Tikkun*, using the pseudonym Yaakov Levado. He saw himself in the prophet's words: "[Isaiah] speaks to two obvious outsider groups in chapter 56, . . . the foreigners of non-Israelite birth, and . . . the eunuchs . . . they are both excluded from the covenantal frame of reference."[26] But Levado found assurance in Isaiah's bold claim that there are other ways to honor God's covenant. Indeed, there are ways to receive and pass on a name, even without progeny. The promise of a monument and a name is *yad vashem* in Hebrew. As we read this text together one afternoon, Rabbi Maggie Wenig said to me, "This is where we get the name—*Yad Vashem*—the Jerusalem memorial to those who were lost in the holocaust, many of whom were killed with their children or before they could bear children. The promise to them is *yad vashem*—a monument and a name, an everlasting name which shall not perish—even if they had no children of their own to remember them."[27]

Isaiah's promise is deeper than embracing a new *category* of people. For too long, categories have been the beginning and end of our ethical deliberations: heterosexuality is good, homosexuality is bad; heterosexuals are good; homosexuals are bad. But categories alone cannot bear the weight of moral discernment. Isaiah spoke not only of "eunuchs" as a category, but of "eunuchs who keep my Sabbath, who do the things that please me." Rabbi Levado is clear that Isaiah's promise goes deeper than category to covenant:

> Gay people cannot be asked to be straight, but they can be asked to "hold fast to the covenant."
>
> Holding fast to the covenant demands that I seek a path toward sanctity in gay sexual life . . .
>
> The complexities generated by a verse in Leviticus need not unravel my commitment to the whole of the Torah.[28]

Krister Stendahl has spoken a similar word within the church: "We all must handle our sexuality responsibly. For Christians, that means sexuality must be expressed according to the principles of fidelity and mutuality. Such responsibility applies equally to those who have come to know themselves as homosexual."[29] Of course, not everyone agrees with the retired bishop of Stockholm. Many church members, including bishops, have protested, saying, "How can we overturn two thousand years of church teaching?" But that same question was once used to uphold slavery in this country and apartheid in South Africa. In a large part of the Christian church, appeals to history and tradition are still used to deny women's ordination. Longevity of tradition does not ensure its faithfulness. It is possible to be wrong for a long time.

But what about the words written down? ***It is the words written down that invite us to see more than the words written down***. It happened when Isaiah heard a word of newness out of exile. It happened when Philip preached the good news of Jesus, though Jesus' name was not in Isaiah's text. The Spirit keeps hovering over the Scripture text and the community text, calling us to roads we'd never imagined! The Spirit keeps calling other Philips to ministries not approved by church authorities in Jerusalem, in Chicago or Nashville, Louisville or Rome. It will be chaotic and confusing for a time—like that day in Caesarea when the Holy Spirit fell upon Cornelius's household *before* Peter even had a chance to baptize them! Luke makes it clear that Peter had been holding onto tradition and church authority too tightly.[30] The baptism of Cornelius does not preempt the baptism of the Ethiopian eunuch; rather, it confirms the validity of that baptism and the Spirit's uncontrollable surprise.

"As they were going along the road, they came to some water." The narrator says this without a hint of surprise as though it's the most normal thing in the world. It's the Ethiopian eunuch who gets our attention: "Look, here is water!" How can it be? The narrator told us at the beginning: this is a "desert" road. There isn't supposed to be any water. "Look, here is water! What is to prevent me from being baptized?"

"EVERYTHING!" we shout—the words written down, centuries of tradition, the fear in our bones. But here is water, water on a desert road. The eunuch doesn't wait for Philip to answer. Could it be that the Holy Spirit had already come upon him? He commands the chariot to stop for he has already heard the good news: "Nothing can prevent me from being baptized!" So it was that both of them went down into the water—the Ethiopian eunuch and Philip—splashing in the scroll of Isaiah.

It could happen in our time. Even in the church. For the words written down urge us to see more than the words written down. Sometimes God makes a river where there isn't one. "Look! Here is water! What is to prevent me from being baptized?" What is to exclude me from the household of God?

> Yes, we'll gather at the river,
> the beautiful, the beautiful river;
> gather with the saints at the river
> that flows by the throne of God.[31]

CHAPTER FIVE

Standing Once More at the River's Edge

From where you are standing now beside the river, you can see that some things have changed since this book was born. Chapters that began as lectures in October 2000 would have been very different if they had come one year later. Some perspectives on these pages may sound askew and out of date. This is bound to happen when our time marks the text. After September 11, 2001, it was difficult to imagine ever preaching again without the ashes of that terrible day covering the pages of the sermon (at least for many preachers in New York City). At Advent Lutheran Church where I'm a member, one long wall of the sanctuary was covered with hundreds of cards, prayers, and children's drawings from all over the country. That Wall of Remembrance stayed with us through the following Easter. In the midst of too much sadness, I was grateful to laugh at a delightful malapropism in a child's note: "I am praying for all of you in New York City. I hope they catch the tourists who did this." Sometimes, we found ourselves arguing with the Scripture texts that were read: "God is our refuge and strength, a very present help in trouble; / Therefore we will not fear though the earth be removed" (Psalm 46:1-2a KJV). But it seemed that the earth had moved, and we were afraid. Other texts assured us, not with promises that seemed too large, but by touching the deep despair that had taken hold of us. Laments assured us with their honesty and anger, like a friend who sits with us when we are grieving and doesn't try to explain our loss.

The Shunammite Woman Interrupts the Ways of War

Not long after we stood weeping beside the Hudson River, war dominated the news. Patriotic bumper stickers soon appeared on trucks and cars and in the windows of Afghani restaurants. American flags sprouted on taxicabs driven by turbaned drivers and reappeared in church chancels after long years in the closet. One minister in a suburb near New York City came to worship one Sunday morning, surprised to see a huge American flag hoisted between the pillars high above the front steps of the church. "God Bless America," which began as a heartfelt collective prayer, started to sound as though the rest of the world was excluded from God's blessing.

In these ongoing days of vengeance and violence, we long for an uprising of persistent Shunammite women to interrupt the cycle of Holy War. Women in Liberia did just that—they interrupted the civil war in their country. One of these women was Leymah Gbowee, president of the women's group at Saint Peter's Lutheran Church in Monrovia. In 2003, she joined with other women, both Christian and Muslim, to found WIPNET, the Women in Peacebuilding Network. The women marched in the streets. They held vigils in churches and mosques. They lay on their bellies on the runway at Monrovia airfield where everyone passing on the highway could see them. "Some say we are an embarrassment to the government," Gbowee said, "but sun and rain are better than the bullets of war . . . We believe God's hands are under us in this effort now. God has turned ears toward us."[1] When the sit-ins began, the president ordered armed men to come with rattans to whip the women. But as their movement grew, he knew that such threats could not stop them:

> Initially, President Taylor refused to meet with the women, but when the power of their movement became evident, he invited them to a meeting. Dressed in sackcloth and ashes to convey their grief for the nation, the women presented their call for a cease-fire and for good-faith negotiations for peace. They refused chairs and protocols of honor, choosing to sit on the floor as a sign of their solidarity with the people. When the president offered them $5000, they refused it, declaring, "Money cannot buy peace!"[2]

As one long-time Lutheran missionary reported in a phone call to the U.S., "Of course, things are bad in Liberia, but there is hope. The Liberian women are protesting for peace."[3] After years of turmoil and violence, a woman, Ellen Johnson Sirleaf, was elected president of Liberia in 2005.

We could spend several Sundays preaching on the stories of *shalom* in 2 Kings, chapter 4. Though it is unlikely that those stories will shape global politics any time soon, they hold up a vision that could encourage ordinary people to keep resisting militarism as the only solution to conflicts.

- 2 Kings 4:1-7—an unending supply of oil for the payment of debts (overflowing into the laps of poor people in Iraq and Nigeria).
- 2 Kings 4:8-37—a mother rising up to insist on life for her children (in Sudan and Chechnya, Palestine and Israel).
- 2 Kings 4:38-41—a poisoned pot of stew made edible (an end to the lethal spraying of Colombian farmers' fields in the U.S. war on drugs).
- 2 Kings 4:42-44—and barley loaves to feed a hundred with some left over (passed out in Darfur and Gaza, in poor rural counties and inner cities across our country).

The Rich Man Keeps Looking for Loopholes

The economic realities that shaped our encounter with Jesus and the rich man would now be marked by the outrageous greed and deception that caused the collapse of Enron and other corporations in 2002. Tax cuts for the wealthiest Americans have, no doubt, created more millionaires than *Barron's* magazine predicted in the year 2000. It is impossible to anticipate whether the stock market will be up or down by the time you are reading this sentence. While the National Council of Churches and many denominational leaders have spoken passionately about the growing gap between the rich and the poor, their voices have been barely audible in the public media. Television, radio, newspapers, and the Internet paid far more attention to Christian voices condemning abortion, gay marriage, and stem cell research. Sam Brownback, an influential senator well regarded by the Christian right, has made it clear that economics is not a pressing concern for ordinary people. While he was still a representative, he made this clear on the floor of the House:

> Mr. Speaker, as I travel my district in eastern Kansas and talk to people back home, I ask them, do they think the biggest problems we face as a nation, are they moral or are they economic? Are they the problems associated with the economy or problems associated with values? And I will get in almost every crowd 8 or 9 to 1 that will say the problems are moral rather than they are economic we are facing.[4]

How did "the economy" become so thoroughly separated from "values"? In his book *What's the Matter with Kansas?* Thomas Frank describes events that transformed his home state of Kansas from the radical rural populism of the 1930s to the reactionary politics of the 1990s. This reactionary climate led to "the 1999 decision by the State Board of Education to delete references to macroevolution and the age of the earth from the state's science standards."[5] Support for teaching creationism was, however, not the only winner. Kansans not only voted to get God back into the schools, but approved economic policies that have changed not only Kansas but the larger landscape:

> Over the last three decades they have smashed the welfare state, reduced the tax burden on corporations and the wealthy, and generally facilitated the country's return to a nineteenth-century pattern of wealth distribution. Thus the primary contradiction of the backlash: it is a working-class movement that has done incalculable, historic harm to working-class people.[6]

"None of what I have described here would make sense," Frank writes, "were it not for a critical rhetorical move: *the systematic erasure of the economic*" (italics added).[7] How can those of us who preach bring "moral" and "economic" together again? Economic justice runs like a mighty river throughout the pages of the Bible. For Christians, the "erasure of the economic" dries that river to a trickle. Those of us who preach need to find ways to put flesh and blood on the word *economics*, a word that often seems far too theoretical. Economics may be measured in statistics and percentages, but economics is about people. Preaching about economics must be as real as boarded up stores in rural North Dakota and farm foreclosure sales in Kansas, as shocking as homeless families being housed in an abandoned jail in New York City and a woman dying of asthma because she has no health insurance. The wealth-poverty gap must be as stark as a poor man named Lazarus covered with sores waiting for crumbs from a rich man's table. Hard as it is to talk about wealth and poverty, we need to invite Jesus and the camel back to church more often.

The Ethiopian Eunuch Returns to the River

One thing has not changed much, except in intensity. The debates over homosexuality are going strong within the churches and the larger culture. At least part of the increased intensity is the result of what many hail as long-awaited justice for gay and lesbian people. In the brief, two-year span of 2002–2004, the

Supreme Court ruled sodomy laws in Texas unconstitutional; the Reverend V. Gene Robinson, a gay Episcopal priest in a committed relationship, was consecrated as Bishop of the Diocese of New Hampshire; and gay marriage was legalized in Massachusetts. In response to what some political leaders called "activist judges," the Senate and the House of Representatives attempted to pass an amendment to the Constitution banning gay marriage. Though congressional efforts failed, eleven states passed amendments prohibiting gay marriage in the elections of 2004. And many denominations continue to be consumed with debates about blessing same-gender relationships and ordaining gay men and lesbians.

Debates in the larger culture often shape ecclesiastical debates rather than the other way around. In listening to debates on the floor of Congress, on talk radio shows and within many churches, a lopsided interpretive principle has taken hold: Everything the Bible says about sex must be *taken literally*, but everything the Bible says about wealth must be *taken with a grain of salt*. In an unabashedly partisan election-year book, radio host Garrison Keillor seemed to confirm Senator Brownback's distinction between "moral" and "economic" (though from a different perspective):

> Republicans are troubled by homosexuality and can't figure out how not to think about it. Hunger and homelessness don't get their attention but the sight of two women kissing gets Republicans all buzzed, what a porch light does for moths.[8]

If you're a Democrat you're probably nodding—and laughing about the moths. Exit polls indicate that this sexual porch light was a decisive factor in the 2004 elections. We do not have to agree with Keillor to acknowledge that, for many, morality is all about sex but cannot touch money. How can we invite people back to the river to discover that the texts of the Bible, including texts about sexuality, were marked by time? Such an understanding does not mean abandoning the Bible; rather, it means getting back to the Bible in all of its fullness and untamability. How did the Bible itself reinterpret words that were written down? We might begin by engaging in some lively conversations with Saint Paul who wasn't afraid to change his mind on matters of eschatology or to admit he sometimes had no word from the Lord on matters of sexuality.

Two Parts Intertwined: Marking and Being Marked

You may be saying to yourself and to me, "Well, who gets to decide how the Bible should be interpreted? Some say it's mainly against sex; others say wealth. Some say it promotes war; others call for non-violence." We must always remember that marking time includes two intertwined realities: our time marks the text *and* the text marks our time. The events and experiences of our time in history bring new insights into the biblical texts: we hear and understand them in ways that were not possible before. But the text continues to have its own voice, a voice that speaks across the ages marking our own time. We cannot bend the text to say something against its will. Consider one example in interpreting the wondrous words from John's prologue:

> In the beginning was the Word, and the Word was with God, and the Word was God. He was in the beginning with God. All things came into being through him, and without him not one thing came into being. What has come into being in him was life, and the life was the light of all people. The light shines in the darkness, and the darkness did not overcome it. (John 1:1-5)

The Word is clearly a person rather than an idea. This becomes clear when John says, "And the Word became flesh and lived among us . . . " (John 1:14a). By the end of the prologue the Word is identified as Jesus Christ. How is that Word heard in our time? On September 11, 2002, President Bush spoke in New York City with the Statue of Liberty lit up behind him:

Ours is the cause of human dignity: freedom guided by conscience and guarded by peace. This ideal of America is the hope of all mankind. That hope drew millions to this harbor. That hope still lights our way. And the light shines in the darkness. And the darkness will not overcome it. May God bless America.[9]

Though the president does not name John's gospel, those who know this Scripture text heard almost the exact words of the prologue. But John's words have a very different meaning in the president's speech. The hope that "drew millions to this harbor" is the light that shines in darkness. Perhaps some understood him to say that America itself is the light because of how the speech ended: "And the light shines in darkness. And the darkness will not overcome it. May God bless America." Note that John's past tense has been changed to future—something will happen in the future, not something has happened in the past. The biblical text that points to Jesus Christ as light of the world has been replaced by America.

A different hearing of John's text came almost four years after that speech in the midst of the war in Iraq. Tom Fox, a member of the Christian Peacemaker Team, was abducted along with three other members of the CPT. His murdered body was found on a Baghdad street on March 9, 2006. Doug Pritchard, codirector of CPT, wrote a moving tribute about Tom's last journey home from Iraq to Dover Air Force Base. Since the bodies of Iraqi detainees who die in U.S. custody are also flown to Dover for autopsies, Tom's coffin was placed beside a detainee's coffin on the plane. Tom accompanied an Iraqi detainee in death, just as he had done so often in life. Beth Pyles, a member of the Christian Peacemaker Team in Iraq, sat vigil with Tom's coffin at Anaconda air base and accompanied his body out onto the tarmac as his coffin was loaded on the plane.

At Tom's departure Beth Pyles read out from the gospel of John, "The light shines in the darkness and the darkness did not overcome it."[10]

Tom Fox was not the light. He never claimed to be nor did others claim this about him. A press release, written the day after his death, pointed to the source of CPT commitment: "Each of our teammates has responded to Jesus' prophetic call to live out a nonviolent alternative to the cycle of violence and revenge."[11] Jesus' call guided Tom Fox and his teammates in the midst of violence and war. When Beth Pyles read John 1:5 beside Tom Fox's coffin, John's meaning remained intact: Jesus Christ is the light that shines in darkness and the darkness did not overcome it. The text stays in past tense as John wrote it, giving assurance and comfort to those who remembered Tom Fox. The darkness did not overcome the light of Christ even in the face of abduction and death.

We are called to remember both parts of the interpretative conversation: the text marks our time and our time marks the text. Only when both are remembered and honored can God's untamable texts find meaning in the midst of our changing lives.

A Book That Is Always Unfinished

This book will always be unfinished and out of date—a bit like the Bible. Remember the ending of John's gospel?

> Now Jesus did many other signs in the presence of his disciples, which are not written in this book. But these are written so that you may come to believe that Jesus is the Messiah, the Son of God, and that through believing you may have life in his name. (John 20:30-31)

What more needs to be said? Close the book. But that was not the end. Chapter 21 begins as though the ending had never been written: "After these things, Jesus showed himself again to the disciples by the Sea of Tiberius." This postscript to John's gospel is rather odd. We hear a familiar fishing story—but shouldn't it come at the beginning? We gather with Jesus and the disciples for breakfast over a charcoal fire—are we supposed to remember

Peter standing by the charcoal fire in the courtyard? We listen as Jesus bids Peter, "Follow me"—but hadn't Peter been called long before, on another day beside the sea? Just when we thought the story was over, Jesus comes once more, telling us the story is never over.

We're still preaching in the postscript. You and I will keep writing this unfinished book in each particular time and place. Time will mark the text in different ways for each of us, even though we are each given the same number of hours in a day. For me, 8:46 a.m., September 11th has a different meaning than it does for my mother, brother, and sister living in small Iowa towns. Our task is not to update the Bible, but to open up a hermeneutical space in which life itself serves to explain the text, a space in which time and text are in lively conversation with each other.

Two months after the towers were attacked, Pastor Heidi Neumark engaged in this kind of lively conversation when she preached at the installation of the bishop of the Evangelical Lutheran Church in America. The preacher faced daunting challenges that often come on such an occasion: the need to address not only those gathered in Rockefeller Chapel but thousands more on streaming video; the ecumenical breadth of the church represented by bishops, patriarchs, and presidents from other faith communions; the passionate concern of the new bishop for ministry in the city while not forgetting thousands of Lutherans who live in rural communities. All of that would have been hard enough, but it was November of 2001, barely two months after the towers were attacked. Pastor Neumark focused on the reading from Isaiah 52: "How beautiful upon the mountains / are the feet of the messenger who announces peace, / who brings good news . . . Break forth together into singing, / you ruins of Jerusalem" (vv. 7a, 8a). The preacher looked at the city of Jerusalem laid waste, its temple in ruins, most of its citizens taken into exile. The text marked our fearful time even as our time marked the text:

> The world-renowned city that seemed invincible, attacked and capsized by terror. Towers collapsed in rubble, bronze temple

pillars broken into pieces, the glorious architectural feat and economic seat in the great city, crashed and burning.

Jerusalem 587—New York 9/11.

. . . .

Survivors in exile from all that was expected and secure. Displaced people without foothold or language, wondering where is the Word that failed to stay this chaos, as tons of paper and all the words scatter and dissolve in ash.

We don't even have the alphabet.

Jerusalem 587—New York 9/11.[12]

Neumark opened up a hermeneutical space in which similarity could be imagined. The text is no longer back there or out there. It is here. It is now. She not only allowed the text to mark our time but also brought our experience back to the ravaged city of Jerusalem and to those who were left behind in the city. She marked the text with our similitudes:

The captain of the guard left some of the poorest people of the land to be vinedressers and tillers of the soil (2 Kings 25:12)— forsaken farmers left behind in the ruined city. So there, in what was considered the waste places of Jerusalem, you had a blend of North Dakota and the South Bronx all in one. A first-call delight![13]

We hadn't fully seen those who had been left behind when others were carried into exile. The preacher brought the farmers of North Dakota and the poorest people of the South Bronx together in the ravaged city so we could see Jerusalem and understand the text itself as never before.

Scripture needs preaching, and preaching is not only for the sake of the church but bold testimony proclaimed for the sake of the world. God's living water cannot be bottled up. The water must flow or it becomes stagnant. The manna cannot be hoarded or it will go bad. God inspired the prophet Ezekiel to see that the word of life cannot be contained inside the temple—or we could add, inside the church. In a glorious vision, Ezekiel is brought around to the front of the temple where he sees water flowing out under the temple doors. He wades in the water. It is up to his ankles, then to his knees, then up to his waist and his neck— finally he has to swim for the water has become a great river. The river flows toward the east and wherever it enters stagnant waters, they are made fresh. Fish come to life. Trees on the banks of the river are lush and green. "And everything will live where the river goes" (see Ezekiel 47:1-9).

What a wondrous vision! The water spills out over the baptismal font, drenching the minister and the acolyte holding the worship book. The pages of the book will never close quite well enough again, crinkled with holy water. The water runs down the center aisle soaking the new carpet, then out under the church doors and into the streets: "And everything will live where the river goes . . . On the banks, on both sides of the river, there will grow all kinds of trees for food . . . Their fruit will be for food, and their leaves for healing" (Ezekiel 47:9a, 12).

At the very end of the Bible, we return once more to the river. John of Patmos borrowed Ezekiel's vision for the last chapter of the book of Revelation:

> Then the angel showed me the river of the water of life, bright as crystal, flowing from the throne of God and of the Lamb through the middle of the street of the city. On either side of the river is the tree of life with its twelve kinds of fruit, producing its fruit each month; and the leaves of the tree are for the healing of the nations. (Revelation 22:1-2)

John's vision is even more expansive than Ezekiel's, for the leaves of Revelation expand to include "the healing of *the nations*." Like biblical visions, preaching points not to itself but moves out under the doors of the church and into the wider world.

The last page of this book is blank, a space where your sermons will continue to mark time in your particular place. God's living word invites us again and again to return to the river where preacher and people will hear words they have never heard before though the text has been read a hundred times. The promise remains as certain as it was when God's people marked time at the Jordan:

Surely, this commandment that I am commanding you today is not too hard for you, nor is it too far away. It is not in heaven, that you should say, "Who will go up to heaven for us, and get it for us so that we may hear it and observe it?" Neither is it beyond the sea, that you should say, "Who will cross to the other side of the sea for us, and get it for us so that we may hear it and observe it?" No, the word is very near to you; it is in your mouth and in your heart for you to observe. (Deuteronomy 30:11-14)

CHAPTER SIX

Sermons Preached at the River's Edge

Fragments (John 6:3, 5-13)

This sermon was preached on September 13, 2001, when there seemed to be no words to say. The Union seminary community had gathered in chapel on Tuesday when the towers fell, a time for prayers, anguished feelings, silence, and weeping. On Thursday, we came to the table for our weekly Communion service. John's account of the feeding of the 5,000 is often understood as a Eucharistic text. I heard the textual detail of "fragments" in a different way because of the events of that week.

"Gather up the fragments left over," said Jesus, **"so that nothing may be lost."**

We have been trying to do that since Tuesday. Trying to find meaning where there is none. Trying to make pieces fit together that are forever broken. Trying to see the skyline as we remembered it. Trying to gather up the fragments. Some of you hadn't even attended your first class at Union before it was cancelled on Tuesday.

I have not been able to gather the fragments into any meaningful whole. I've turned to the Psalms to cry and rage and I've stood with Jesus weeping as he looks out over the city. But it was the fragments that led me to John's gospel, to the story of broken bread and fish. "And from the fragments of the five barley loaves, left by those who had eaten, they filled twelve baskets." (Evidently, they had eaten all the fish!) John doesn't tell us what the disciples did with all those pieces of bread. Perhaps, after all these centuries, they're still being passed out, even today.

Fragments—that's all I have today, but I have been assured that fragments are something rather than nothing.

Fragment: On Tuesday someone set up a TV in "The Pit," Union's town square and meeting place. That afternoon, Jill Lum brought her daughter to school for the first time. Only four days old, the tiny girl slept soundly, completely unaware of our need to see and touch her. Jill set the baby carrier on the table so we could gather around—amazed at fingernails so perfectly formed at such a young age. A wondrous miracle of life while images of death came at us from the television a few feet away. A double-exposed photograph. How can we gather up the fragments that tell us life goes on even when we fear it will not?

Fragment: Yesterday, I received an e-mail from my friend Viola Raheb in Bethlehem, passing on a letter from her brother Mitri. She is director of Lutheran schools on the West Bank and he is pastor of the Evangelical Christmas Lutheran Church in Bethlehem. (Did you know there were Palestinian Lutherans?) They expressed their deep sorrow and profound grief for the victims of this tragic attack. They also shared their fear and dismay: "Unfortunately, the media has shown scenes of a few Palestinians celebrating this tragedy. We want you to know that these few do not speak for or represent the entire Palestinian people . . ." I give thanks to God that Farid Esack has come from South Africa to be with us this semester to teach "The World of Islams," to talk with us in the hallways, to read from the Koran as he did two days ago when we gathered here raw with fear and grief. Already we have heard of news of Muslim people being attacked, of mosques and schools marred with hateful threats. What can we do as people of faith, primarily Christian, across the street from Jewish Theological Seminary, in a city increasingly Muslim? How can we gather up the fragments of understanding and hope across our different religious traditions?

Fragment: We have seen the human spirit rising from the ashes: the unfathomable courage of ordinary people—a man carrying a woman who couldn't walk down fifty-four stories to safety. "I only knew his name was Louie," she said. Firefighters, police, and EMTs risking their lives to save others, refusing to give up hope, searching and digging even now while we worship. Did you see the long lines around the block at Saint Luke's hospital on 114th Street?—too many people eager to give blood. More volunteers than there are jobs. "Come back tomorrow." How can we gather up fragments of determination and courage to face together all that must be done to mend our city?

Fragment: Waking or sleeping, we cannot get the towers out of our minds—the towers that shaped the skyline and helped us find our bearings. The towers where I stood with my mom and dad from an Iowa farm, looking down in wonder at the toy buses far below, at the city spread out to the north, at the lady with the lamp in the harbor. The solid, shining towers collapsing into dust. But we knew without speaking that the towers were not empty: they were filled with people. From now on we cannot speak as we have spoken before. Never again can we use the language of "surgical strikes" or "collateral damage." From now on, we must speak of people. How can we gather up the fragments—the photos of the missing—and extend our compassion to those beyond our shores whose faces will never be posted on the walls and lampposts of our city?

Fragment: Yesterday, some of you headed downtown, not knowing what to do. The blood banks were filled and the Red Cross didn't know what to do with you. So you went where people were gathering—Union Square Park. There, you prayed and sang and talked with those who were searching for loved ones. Soon forty others joined you—people you'd never met. It was a ministry of presence where there were no explanations. Fragments of songs and prayers connecting with the fragments brought by others, transforming a public space into a sanctuary of solace and grace. How can we at Union, with all of our own problems, be the people God is calling us to be in this city at this time?

Gathering up the fragments may be all we can do now because any larger meaning eludes us. With God's help, we must shape meaning together in the days to come. Fragments, that's all we have. But fragments aren't nothing—excuse the grammar, but it's true. Dietrich Bonhoeffer, who once studied and worshiped in this place, talked about fragments in a letter to his friend Eberhard Bethge, written from prison in February of 1944. He acknowledged that some fragments are fit only for "the dustbin of history." But others, completed by God, come together in the manner of a *fugue*—the separate fragmentary notes creating something we cannot yet hear or even imagine:

> If our life is but the remotest reflection of such a fragment, if we accumulate at least for a short time, a wealth of themes and weld them into a harmony in which the great counterpoint is maintained from start to finish . . . we will not bemoan the fragmentariness of our life, but rather rejoice in it.[1]

I know . . . we aren't yet ready to rejoice. But it is my prayer that we will honor the fragments of hope and grief, courage and despair, and offer them all to God. Bonhoeffer lifted up the fragments of his own weariness in Tegel prison: "I'm still very tired," he writes, "and unfortunately that hinders productive work considerably."[2] You may already have discovered that this is true also for you: there is a fatigue that weighs you down even when you go to bed long before midnight. Be gentle with yourself and with each other in the days ahead.

Bonhoeffer closed his letter to his friend with fragments about ordinary things:

> What is the food like? When do you get leave? When are we going to baptize your boy? When shall we be able to talk together again, for hours at a time? Good-bye, Eberhard. Keep well! . . . God bless you. I think of you every day.
>   Your faithful Dietrich[3]

God bless each one of you, too, and gather up the fragments of your days.

In God We Trust (Revelation 18:10b-20)

The months immediately following 9/11 were marked by precipitous drops in the stock market and a barrage of corporate scandals. As is often true during a time of crisis, there was increased interest in the book of Revelation. This interest was fueled by the apocalyptic language of good versus evil in the public square, as well as the popular Left Behind series of novels. While this sermon doesn't address the novels, it seeks to lift up economic issues often neglected in books that focus on predicting the end times. This sermon was preached in the summer of 2002 at the Great Auditorium, Ocean Grove, New Jersey.

Have you seen GOD on the highway? You know what I mean? Those semi-trailer trucks with G.O.D. in huge letters on the side. The first time I saw one I couldn't believe my eyes. GOD on a truck! Then I read the smaller print: Guaranteed Overnight Delivery. GOD on the highway carrying who-knows-what. Not long ago I saw a double-trailer in New York City—G.O.D. written twice going down Broadway. So if it ever turns out that we can't say "under God" in the Pledge of Allegiance at least God will be on the road. I'm not sure what will happen to our money. Will we have to reprint our bills to get rid of "In God We Trust"?

What does it mean to call ourselves "one nation under God"? What difference does it make that a dollar bill says "In God We Trust" over the word *one*? These are important questions for those of us who call ourselves Christians. They are pressing questions, urgent questions at this moment of history. For many believers these are apocalyptic times, the final battle between Good and Evil. This is a time for many to turn to the book of Revelation: God's promise of a new heaven and a new earth, a time when all tears will be wiped away, a time when we will gather at the river that flows from the throne of God. It is probably true that more has been written about Revelation than any other book of the Bible. Go into any Christian bookstore and you'll see shelf after shelf of books on the end time, the battle of Armageddon, the 144,000 standing before the throne of God. Many of these books offer clear interpretations of the strange symbols in this book: the seven candlesticks, the seven seals, the seven bowls—and the Great Beast. Down through history the Beast has been named and renamed many times. Almost always in American history, the Beast has been an enemy of the United States: the Soviet Union, Communist Cuba, and now, Iraq.

But in all these certain predictions an urgent message of Revelation has been almost completely forgotten. Exiled on the isle of Patmos, John was writing urgent words to Christians threatened by oppression and persecution under the power of Rome. Those who read this letter understood that John was talking about Rome when he said "Babylon." The book builds and builds through seventeen chapters until it rises to outrage in chapter 18, announcing the fall of Babylon. The sin of the great city has everything to do with economics, with wealth and materialism. But because Babylon is called a "whore" many have assumed that the sins of the city were primarily sexual. Our churches—most of them in this country—have spent many years talking about sex. We have debated and studied and made pronouncements about sex, but we have been deceived into silence about greed.

For John the excessive wealth of the Roman Empire was a clear sign of idolatry. Listen, once more, to his strong words in Revelation 18:10—

> Alas, alas, the great city,
> Babylon, the mighty city!
> For in one hour your judgment has come.

Then, he gets specific. Those who mourn the fall of Babylon/ Rome are weeping for the loss of material goods, a drop in their portfolios. We can imagine ourselves walking through the mall, peering into every shop window, as John lays Babylon's goods before our eyes:

And the merchants of the earth weep and mourn for
her, since no one buys their cargo anymore, cargo of gold,
silver, jewels and pearls, fine linen, purple, silk and scarlet,
all kinds of scented wood, all articles of ivory, all articles
of costly wood, bronze, iron and marble, cinnamon, spice,
incense, myrrh, frankincense, wine, olive oil, choice flour
and wheat, cattle and sheep, horses and chariots, slaves—and
human lives.

. . . .

Alas, alas, the great city,
  Where all who had ships at sea
  grew rich by her wealth.
For in one hour she has been laid waste. (vv. 11-13, 19b)

What might John say in our own time?

Alas, alas, the great nation!
They traded and speculated, they established companies that
    were not,
    they laid up for themselves treasures—gold and silver and
    fine art,
they built homes, one more extravagant than the next,
    and laid up bank accounts far beyond these shores;
they sold their stocks for millions
    while those who had little ended up with nothing.
Their greed knows no end and the heaping up of wealth no
    bounds.
See how they parade in the marketplace,
    putting their name on stadium and tower!
And on Sunday morning they enter the sanctuary, praising
    God,
    and giving alms that cannot be missed.
"Come out of her," the seer cried,
    "and take part in her sins no more."

But those who hear the words know that John isn't talking to
them for they have been to the Wednesday morning Bible study
in downtown Houston. John is speaking about the Evil Axis:
Iraq, Iran, and North Korea.

Of course, we don't know what John would say to us in the United States at this time in history. But we do know what Alan Greenspan, Federal Reserve chairman, said in July 2002: "an infectious greed seemed to grip much of our business community . . . It is not that humans have become any more greedy than in generations past. It is that the avenues to express greed had grown so enormously."[4] It isn't only Enron or WorldCom or Tyco or Andersen or their CEOs. Something has happened to me, perhaps also to you. Greed has a trickle-down effect. When the markets were soaring, I opened my pension report with glee to see how well I was doing! Now, I don't even dare to open the envelopes.

Perhaps it is easier to think of Revelation as a book condemning seductive sex and foreign enemies. Confronting economic inequities is too complicated, too political, and, well, when economics means my money, it is just too personal. But if we erase economics from the call to discipleship, we forsake God's call from the beginning to the end of the Bible—words spoken to wanderers in the wilderness, Isaiah's words about true fasting, and Amos's strong plea on behalf of the poor:

> Hear this, you that trample on the needy,
>   and bring to ruin the poor of the land,
> saying, "When will the new moon be over
>   so that we may sell grain,
> and the sabbath,
>   so that we may offer wheat for sale?
> We will make the ephah small and the shekel great,
>   and practice deceit with false balances,
>   buying the poor for silver
>   and the needy for a pair of sandals . . ." (Amos 8:4-6)

Jesus' ministry was shaped by the prophets' passionate pleas. In his first public sermon, Jesus set forth his agenda based on a text from the prophet Isaiah. The first item on that Spirit-born agenda was to preach good news to the poor. Jesus was seldom ambiguous about the dangers of wealth, whether in his parables or his encounters with people such as the rich ruler. Running like a stream throughout Scripture is a persistent call to remember the widow and the orphan, to leave grain for sojourners at the edge of the field, to act with fairness in the marketplace, to share your bread with the hungry, and to bring the homeless poor into your house. The holy river flowing from the throne of God in the last chapter of Revelation has been fed by justice streams from the whole Bible.

Sisters and brothers, we can't wade in that water without getting our money wet!

If we listened more closely to the whole book of Revelation, we'd worry about greed as passionately as we worry about sex. We'd be as committed to naming the demonic powers of materialism within as we are about naming the Beast outside our borders. We'd raise pressing questions about tax cuts that benefit the wealthiest of our citizens while the lines at soup kitchens and food pantries wind around the block. We can't wade in the water of life without getting our money wet.

Yet John's purpose in writing this strange book was not to make people feel guilty or give in to despair. Above all, his message was a strong word to keep on keeping on in the midst of an oppressive and greedy Empire. God is with you now, says John. God promises to strengthen you and me against the seductive power of the Empire. Though some Christians dwell on God suddenly drawing believers up to heaven, John pictures the heavenly city coming *down to earth.* "See, the home of God is among mortals," he cries. "He will dwell with them as their God; / they will be [God's] peoples, / and God himself will be with them" (Revelation 21:3b).

God didn't promise Guaranteed Overnight Delivery to Christians living under the power of Rome. The promise to them was the same as God's promise to us: I will be with you today, tomorrow, and until the end of time. Our faithfulness will not be guaranteed by printing "In God We Trust" on our money, but by trusting God enough to get our money wet.

Turning Letters into Laws (1 Corinthians 7:29-31)

During Epiphany of 2003 the Epistle readings appointed in the lectionary came from 1 Corinthians, often dropping people into the middle of a chapter without setting the stage. The sermon I preached at Advent Lutheran Church in Manhattan on the last Sunday of January 2003 was later adapted for this article in a newsletter for The Network, a group supporting the ordination of non-celibate gay and lesbian people in the ELCA.

During these Sundays of Epiphany, we're reading through portions of Paul's first letter to the Corinthians. Sometimes the lectionary drops us into the middle of a chapter without giving us a chance to get our bearings. If you were here last Sunday, you probably know what I mean. We jumped into the middle of the sixth chapter. After reading about fornication and food, the reader closed the book and said, "May God give us some understanding of *that* word." People seemed uncertain whether they should say, "Thanks be to God!"

Today we've received another strange reading from 1 Corinthians. Though I had several sermons in my files about Jesus calling the fishermen, I remembered what I often tell my students in preaching class, "If you read a difficult text aloud in worship you can't pretend nobody heard it. You're called to preach on it." So take the Gospel reading home and read it during the week, but this morning, we turn to the reading from 1 Corinthians, chapter 7.

Like last Sunday, the lectionary has started in the middle of the chapter without any background: " . . . from now on, let even those who have wives be as though they had none." Well, that must be shocking news for those of you who have been married forty years. I can see that it's also disheartening for those of you who just got married. What does it mean for husbands to live as though they have no wives? How should they act and what should they do? Note that Paul doesn't say, "Let even those who have husbands be as though they had none." This omission sets up a perplexing situation: the wives still think they have husbands but the husbands are living as though they have no wives! (Well, you have to understand Paul's context.)

Or consider Paul's words earlier in this same chapter: "To the unmarried and the widows I say that it is well for them to remain unmarried as I am." So if you're coming to this church hoping to find an eligible partner, forget it! Stay single—like Paul. Of course he does add, "It is better to marry than to be aflame with passion." (But again, we have to understand Paul's context . . .)

In recent publications, in meetings organized to oppose the work of the sexuality task force, and in letters to *The Lutheran* magazine, someone almost always says, "We don't need this study. The Bible is absolutely clear about sex and marriage." Are they thinking about 1 Corinthians 7 when they say such things? If so, then Paul's advice to the Corinthian church might become part of a sexuality statement adopted by the next church assembly: "Persons who are unmarried or widowed should not marry again, for as Saint Paul writes, 'I say it is well for them to remain unmarried as I am.'" (Of course this is silly—I'm taking Paul out of context.)

Now some will hear 1 Corinthians, chapter 7, as one more reason to stop reading Paul altogether. Others will say, "It's confusing but it's in the Bible and that's all I need to know." Both positions fail to listen closely enough to what Paul's saying in his letter. From reading his words, it's clear that there are problems in Corinth. In the first chapter Paul says that he has received word about quarrels within the young church—some say, "I belong to Paul"; others "I belong to Apollos or Peter" or "I belong to Christ" (see v. 12). This was long before people said, "I belong to the Network" or "I belong to Word Alone."[5] Paul cares about this young church in the bustling harbor city. "I am not writing this to make you ashamed," he says, "but to admonish you as my beloved children" (1 Corinthians 4:14).

When we get to chapter 7, Paul begins to respond not to verbal reports brought by Chloe's people, but to specific questions that had come to him in a letter: "Now concerning the matters about which you wrote," he begins . . . and the whole chapter is about sex. He quotes from their letter: "It is well for a man not to touch a woman." But Paul doesn't agree. Though he's not too positive about either sex or marriage, he argues with those who claimed that Christians had become completely spiritual people. At times he seems to be saying that the only good thing about marriage is to keep a man or woman from sinning—that is, there's nothing good in marriage itself. However, to those who taught that a man should never touch a woman under any circumstances, Paul affirms sexual expression within marriage:

> The husband should give to his wife her conjugal rights, and
> likewise the wife to her husband . . . Do not deprive one
> another except perhaps by agreement for a set time, to devote
> yourselves to prayer, and then come together again, so that
> Satan may not tempt you because of your lack of self-control.
> (1 Corinthians 7:3, 5)

Now we might want to say some more positive things about sexuality and marriage besides curbing temptation, but Paul was responding to the Corinthians' letter—not ours.

And this is a very important distinction. Paul wasn't trying to answer our questions. He wasn't writing systematic theology or a social statement on Christian sexual ethics. He was writing a letter, a letter addressed to particular concerns of Corinthian believers who were struggling to live their lives in light of the good news of Jesus Christ. Paul admits that he doesn't have all the answers. That's what's so disarming about Paul in this chapter. We can hear his struggle in the verses that come just before today's reading. He turns to another question they've asked him: "Now concerning virgins," he says in verse 25, "I have no command of the Lord, but I give my opinion . . . " Bishop Krister Stendahl says that Paul was "the last preacher in Christendom who had the guts to say that."[6] Many people who speak about sex, especially about homosexuality, claim to speak with divine authority. It may be far more honest to say, with Paul, "I have no command from the Lord, but I give my opinion…*The thought of two men in bed together makes me sick. Why would a woman want to be with another woman? What do they do? I don't even want to talk about sex—it's too embarrassing. Other boys in school call me a fag and I'll do anything to prove them wrong. If our church approves gay marriage that demeans me and my wife.*" If people could say, "These are my opinions," that would be a healthy place to begin.

Paul's opinions were shaped by his sense of urgency. He fully expected Jesus to return within his lifetime; indeed, he thought the time would be very soon. His answers to the Corinthians' questions about sex and marriage are shaped by this sense of timing: "Are you bound to a wife? Do not seek to be free. Are you free from a wife? Do not seek a wife. But if you marry, you do not sin, and if a virgin marries, she does not sin. Yet those who marry will experience distress in this life, and I would spare you that" (1 Corinthians 7:27-28). This sense of urgency continues in today's reading: "I mean, brothers and sisters, the appointed time has grown short; from now on, let even those who have wives be as though they had none." He goes on to say the same about those who mourn, those who rejoice, and those who have possessions. Live as though this present age is passing away.

It's impossible to know what Paul would say in answer to *our* questions two thousand years later. He was not answering our questions, but the questions and concerns of particular churches in the century after Jesus' resurrection. If we take Paul's letters as definitive statements on sex and marriage, we misuse the particularity of this letter by turning his words into universal, timeless proscriptions. If we dismiss Paul all together, we miss his concern for the real-life dilemmas people faced in a culture that offered myriad competing claims and values. If we can read his letters *as letters*, we can learn a great deal about what it means to be Christ's church in each particular time and place, including our own.

This week I received a copy of another letter, this one written to Lutheran Christians *in* Saint Paul—but not *by* Saint Paul. The letter came from Peter Rogness, bishop of the Saint Paul Area

Synod. He wrote to tell people that he was removing the sanctions against two congregations in the synod. Saint Paul Reformation and Hosanna Lutheran Churches had been censured for failing to follow church policies in ordaining pastors. Hosanna, a rapidly growing, suburban congregation had called and ordained people on its staff even though they weren't approved by the ELCA. Saint Paul Reformation, an urban congregation, had called and ordained Anita Hill as their pastor after she had served as their "pastoral minister" for several years. While fully qualified for ordination, Pastor Hill is not endorsed by the ELCA because she is living in a committed relationship with another woman. The sanctions precluded members of both congregations from serving on synod council or boards, as officers or on any task forces of the synod.

Yet both congregations continued to be involved in the synod and continued to reach out to their communities. Nothing has changed in official church policy regarding ordination, but Bishop Rogness believes that sanctions against these congregations have become merely punitive, without any larger purpose. Like the Apostle Paul centuries before him, Bishop Rogness was responding to particular situations within the Christian community:

> I believe we need to recognize that the occasional church which steps out of the box may, in the long run, be contributing to the life of the church in ways more constructive than destructive . . .
>
> Flexibility and diversity are needed for effectiveness in mission in a changing world.
>
> I believe it is time to recognize anew that what binds us together as Christ's church is far more central to our common life than are the constitutional infractions of past actions . . . It is time to make clear that our relationship with these congregations is a relationship focused on mission and ministry and not on rules . . .
>
> With affirmation of the life we share and the faithfulness of the God who continues to call us into life together in this church, we pray for the continued guidance of the Spirit as we move confidently into the future.[7]

I think Paul would understand. Bishop Rogness was respond-ing to questions and concerns raised in this time and place. Of course some will surely remind him—and me—that Paul wrote other words that seem to argue against any decision that allows a lesbian woman to serve as pastor. In Romans 1 Paul wrote: "Their women exchanged natural intercourse for unnatural, and in the same way also the men, giving up natural intercourse with women, were consumed with passion for one another" (Romans 1:26b-27a). These words are often cited as the definitive word condemning gay and lesbian relationships though Paul knew nei-ther of those words. Nor did he know the word *homosexual*. When speaking about biblical texts, the argument often goes something like this: Even if we set aside the holiness codes of Leviticus, we must take Romans 1:26-27 as authoritative teaching on sexuality for all time.[8]

But what happened to context and particularity? Well, it's pos-sible to see *context* as important or irrelevant depending on our "opinions." I think it's true for all of us. Those who affirm Paul's prohibitions of homosexuality will acknowledge that his strange teachings in 1 Corinthians 7 need to be taken "in context," but that Romans 1 is a different matter all together. Those who read Paul's teachings in 1 Corinthians 7 as demeaning or absurd for single and married people alike will read that chapter as confir-mation that *everything* Paul said about sexual ethics has to be taken "in context," including Romans 1:26-27.

Of course, Paul did more than give his opinions in 1 Corinthians 7: "To the married I give this command—*not I but the Lord*—that the wife should not separate from her husband (but if she does separate, let her remain unmarried or else be rec-onciled to her husband), and that the husband should not divorce his wife" (vv. 10-11, italics added). Paul is very clear here, as clear as Jesus was when he talked about divorce and remarriage. Yet, as a church, we do not prohibit divorced women and men from being ordained, nor do we "remove them from the roster" if they divorce following ordination. Taking Paul and Jesus seriously, should we then amend church documents govern-ing ordination to add a line similar to the sentence about gay and lesbian people? "Resolved: To amend *Vision and Expectations* by addition: 'Persons who are divorced and remarried are prohibited from ordination in this church.'"9

I don't plan to introduce such a resolution at the next church-wide Assembly; however, such a resolution would be consistent with Scripture and with the teachings of the church for two thousand years. I don't know if Paul would draft such an amendment—he'd probably get more than a little impatient with parliamentary procedures. I think he'd opt for writing a few more letters to congregations struggling to be faithful in confusing times. He might not know what to say to the questions of our own time, but he would, no doubt, have some opinions. But most of all, I think Saint Paul would assure Bishop Rogness and those who belong to congregations throughout the church, that we all belong to Christ. He would probably say what he said long ago to a church he'd never even visited:

> For I am convinced that neither death, nor life, nor angels, nor rulers, nor things present, nor things to come, nor powers, nor height, nor depth, nor anything else in all creation will be able to separate us from the love of God in Christ Jesus our Lord. (Romans 8:38-39)

What the Mighty Might Learn (2 Kings 5:1-14)

This sermon was preached as part of the Lenten Preaching Series at Calvary Church, Memphis, shortly before the United States began bombing Baghdad in March 2003.

Who did you see in this story? There are Naaman the great warrior, and his wife. There's the king who got so upset that he tore his clothes. There's Elisha, the man of God. Who did I leave out?

The servants. Without the servants there would be no story. No cure. No happy ending. Nothing remembered. And this story is remembered through the centuries. Jesus knew it was so familiar that he could refer to Naaman when he preached his first sermon in Nazareth. "There were also many lepers in Israel in the time of the prophet Elisha," Jesus said, "and none of them was cleansed except Naaman the Syrian" (Luke 4:27). Jesus didn't mention the servants—but he wouldn't have known the story without them.

The story in 2 Kings 5 begins with Naaman: "Naaman, commander of the army of the king of Aram, was a great man and in high favor with his master . . ." The narrator gives us a big picture. This is an important man! He is a commander of the king's army. A four-star general. Head of the joint chiefs of staff. In favor with the king. One of the inner circle. Naaman is somebody to reckon with. That's how the narrator begins the story—we have to see that this man is powerful in every way. But then the story takes a turn: "The man, though a mighty warrior, suffered from leprosy." So everything that was said about Naaman shifts in our minds. All the greatness described at the start can't change this one terrible truth: he suffers from leprosy. A mighty warrior, but infected with a disease so terrible that his skin is rotting on his bones.

Then, the narrator brings in another character, very different from the mighty warrior. She is a slave, carried off on a raid into Israel. Mighty warriors were accustomed to such booty—gold, silver, chariots, horses, and slaves. They could have what they wanted. This nameless slave girl had been carried from her home and now serves Naaman's wife. She is as small as Naaman is big. The power he has is power she lacks. Yet she is not silent. "If only my lord were with the prophet who is in Samaria!" she tells her mistress. "He would cure him of his leprosy" (v. 3). Now, why does this young girl care about this man whose army had carried her away from her own family? That's one perplexing question. But here's another: Why do Naaman's wife and Naaman and the king listen to what this slave girl said?

The text doesn't tell us such things—only that the king of Aram gives Naaman permission to set out on the journey to find this prophet. So Naaman goes off with lots of gifts and a letter of introduction from his king. But when the king of Samaria reads the letter, he's distressed to the core. "Am I God, to give death or life, that this man sends word to me to cure a man of his leprosy?" (v. 7b). It doesn't occur to him that he wasn't the center of things! This is between kings—the king of Aram is trying to trick me! (The people in power don't often consider there may be other possibilities.)

Enter Elisha, the prophet: "Stop tearing up your clothes!" he tells the king. You're not the only one around here, you know. "Send the man to me so that he may learn there's a prophet in Israel." With that, the king drops out of the picture, his clothes still ripped to shreds. The mighty warrior and his chariots and horses, and gifts of gold and silver, head to Elisha's house. Oh, this is a great scene. Elisha doesn't even come out of his house! He sends his servant out with a message for Naaman: "Go, wash in the Jordan seven times, . . . and you will be clean." Well, Naaman isn't used to this. He is a man with authority. He is accustomed to speaking with kings, his own and the kings of other nations. Who does this Elisha think he is? You can be sure he has no intention of washing in the muddy Jordan. "Aren't the rivers of Damascus better than all the waters of Israel?" If Israel's prophet is going to *dis* Naaman by not even coming out of his house, then Naaman will *dis* Israel's river! With that outburst, the mighty warrior turns toward home (see vv. 8-13). That would have been the end of it.

Except for the servants. Naaman's servants are horrified with their master's behavior. Do they trust the word of the servant girl in a way the mighty man does not? "Father," they say, "if the prophet had commanded you to do something difficult, would you not have done it? How much more, when all he said to you was, 'Wash, and be clean'?" (v. 13). Ah, they know how to get to their master. Of course, he'd do something difficult. Of course, he had done many difficult things before. He was, after all, a mighty warrior. So he is surely brave enough to wash in a muddy river. With that, he turns around, goes down to the Jordan, and immerses himself in the river seven times. When he comes up out of the water that last time, he looks down at his hands and feet. His flesh is like the flesh of a young boy. None of his servants say, "I told you so."

There would be no story without the servants—the slave girl who remembered God's prophet and the servants who turned Naaman's pride around. The mighty warrior was made whole by the power of God—and by the intervention of the servants. We could simply say it's a wonderful story. An old story. The kind of story you tell around the fire, remembering God's mighty acts among our ancestors. But is there something the mighty might learn from this story?

Our country is a mighty country. By many measurements, we are the mightiest country on earth. We cherish our freedom and our wondrous diversity. Who can match our economic prowess? Even in a falling market, the wealth of the United States exceeds the wealth of the whole developing world. Our country is also a mighty warrior. Who can match our power and might? As of September 2001, there were at least 725 American military bases outside the United States.[10] The military budget for this year [2003] is $396 billion—that's more than the next twenty-five highest-spending countries put together.[11]

Do the mighty have anything to learn?

Do our leaders need to listen to anybody else in the world?

Lately, it seems that we are mighty enough to say no to both these questions. In the past two years we have refused to sign international agreements to protect the environment—even though we produce more destructive gases than any other nation. We are mighty enough to make our own rules. We have protested the establishment of an international criminal court, unless Americans are given special exemptions. We have long withheld our fair share contribution to the United Nations, yet we have insisted that the U.N. and all its member states affirm our desire for war against Iraq. We name those who agree with us our friends, and label all others as our enemies.

Today we stand on the brink of war against the nation of Iraq. Perhaps it seems far too late to be asking questions, yet, even if bombing begins tomorrow or the day after, there are pressing questions that all our might and power cannot silence. What might the mighty learn from other peoples of the world? What are some questions we might ask about our mighty, beloved country?

- How do we have the right to speak of Russian oil and Nigerian oil and Saudi oil and Iraqi oil as "our" oil, as part of "America's petroleum security"? Or as the bumper sticker asks, "How Did *Our* Oil Get in *Their* Sand?"
- Why did the United States show so little commitment to the Earth Summit in Johannesburg, South Africa? Does it matter to us that eighty countries reported per capita incomes lower than they had a decade ago?[12]
- Has our military might made us so arrogant that we no longer want or need to be part of a community of nations?
- What would we learn if we listened to the poorest of the world's people and to the poorest citizens of our own country? Do we care that the number of homeless families in New York City increased so dramatically last summer (2002) that men, women, and their children were housed in an abandoned city jail?

What might the mighty learn if we risked such questions? Naaman would not have been restored to health if he hadn't listened to his servants. Millions of the world's people must feel that our country treats them like servants: sewing our clothes for pennies, drilling our oil, stitching our sneakers, and falling in line whenever we call. Yet it has become all too clear that our military might has not made us more secure. The world would be healthier if our nation could grasp a vision bigger than our military might. Given the superiority and sophistication of our weapons, it's very likely that we will win a war against Iraq. But we will still be sick.

Naaman was a mighty warrior, but all his might could not restore him to health. He would never have been healed if he hadn't listened to those who had no power. Isn't God longing for us to do the same?

No Prayer for Nineveh (Jonah 2:1-12)

This sermon was preached at convocation at Yale Divinity School in the fall of 2004. Though President Bush had declared victory in the war over a year earlier, violence was spreading in many parts of Iraq. The news of the week reported many flare-ups in the city of Mosul. Portions of the sermon in italics were current news releases from the Internet.

How could Jonah pray such beautiful words in the belly of a fish? Does it help to know it was a *large* fish? Surely he didn't have a copy of the *Book of Common Prayer*, 1928 edition. The text does indicate that it took him a while: "Jonah was in the belly of the fish three days and three nights. THEN Jonah prayed to the LORD" (Jonah 1:17b–2:1a, emphasis added). You and I could probably think up a fine prayer if we had three days and three nights. Of course many have insisted that the prayer is a later addition to the text. Jonah didn't think up the prayer. Somebody who had plenty of time wrote it and inserted it here, interrupting the narrative. It's clear that the story could proceed without the prayer, going directly from Jonah being swallowed to Jonah being spit up.

Whether the prayer was there all the time or added later on, here it is. Did someone want to redeem Jonah, to show his change of heart? "I called to the LORD out of my distress," he prayed, "and he answered me" (v. 2). But Jonah hadn't called to the Lord when the storm was raging—it was the supposedly pagan sailors who cried out to the Lord. Jonah hadn't called to the Lord; Jonah had run when the Lord called! In his prayer, Jonah strings together verses from several psalms. We might try it . . .

> The LORD is my shepherd I shall not want . . .
> I lift up my eyes to the hills from whence cometh my help? . . .
> God is our refuge and strength . . .
> The LORD is my light and my salvation . . .
> Yea though I walk through the valley of the shadow of death
>   I will fear no evil . . .
> (See Psalms 23; 27; 46; 121.)

Jonah knew the words. He could sing the hymns by heart. *But he didn't mention Nineveh.* Nineveh, the great city. Capital of Assyria, sacked long before Jonah prayed.

The ruins of Nineveh are now within the city of Mosul in northern Iraq. The Mosque of Younis (that is Jonah) is there, on the left bank of the Tigris River. If you go to www.globalsecurity.org/military/world/ iraq/mosul, you will learn that there is a room inside the mosque that is the prophet Younis' shrine. "On the walls of the room one can see the whale bones."[13]

Of course Jonah wouldn't mention Nineveh. He was trying to forget Nineveh, hoping that God would forget, too.

> As my life was ebbing away,
> I remembered the LORD;
> and my prayer came to you,
> into your holy temple. (Jonah 2:7)

Jonah would rather be in the sanctuary of the great fish than in the streets of that wicked city.

> Those who worship vain idols
> forsake their true loyalty.
> But I with the voice of thanksgiving
> will sacrifice to you;
> what I have vowed I will pay. (vv. 8-9)

Have the readers forgotten? It was the sailors who offered a sacrifice to the Lord. It was the sailors who made vows. In case we've forgotten, Phyllis Trible reminds us: "Between the genuine worship of the sailors and the genuine repentance of the Ninevites comes counterfeit piety from loquacious Jonah."[14]

I called to the Lord . . .
    out of the belly of Sheol *I* cried . . .
I went down . . .
I remembered the Lord . . .
I will sacrifice to you . . .
What *I* have vowed *I* will pay . . .
I, I, I, I . . . I-Yi-Yi-Yi-Yi!

Jonah was grateful to be saved from the watery deep, from the weeds that wrapped around his head. "Deliverance belongs to the LORD!" he cried in verse 9. (My deliverance is what he meant.) God had heard enough of this liturgy. The Lord spoke to the fish and it vomited Jonah out upon the dry land. The text doesn't say where Jonah landed, but he had some walking to do!

> Nineveh was not on the coast, not in Israel. Nineveh was inland in what is now Iraq. The ruins of Nineveh are within the city of Mosul, third largest city in the country. Several US military bases are there: Camp Performance, Camp Leader, Camp Strike, Camp Top Gun. "Camp Performance offers a café with a variety of both American and Iraqi cuisine including the Sunday special of a double cheeseburger with fries."[15]

"The Word of the Lord came to Jonah a second time saying, 'Get up, go to Nineveh, that great city . . .' "(3:1-2, italics added). When Jonah forgot the name, God remembered. So it was that Jonah picked himself up and made his way to the great city. After a day's walk, he proclaimed God's message. Like the sailors, the people of Nineveh believed. Everyone fasted—from the king to the cattle. Not only that, but everyone dressed in sackcloth—from the king to the cattle. It must have been quite a sight, all those cattle wearing sackcloth!

Jonah never prays for "Nineveh." God is the one who remembers the vast city. Jonah gets out of town as fast as he can. He builds a booth outside the city, a little chapel where he watches and waits to see what will happen. Perhaps God will yet destroy the city (though Jonah fears this isn't likely). For Jonah knew that God wasn't fair, and he had told God so: "I knew that you are a gracious God and merciful, slow to anger, and abounding in steadfast love . . ." Jonah knows that God will spare the city and it makes him so mad he wants to die. Then God appoints a bush—even as God had appointed a large fish. Safe in the shade of the leafy bush, safe from the burning wind, safe as he felt in the belly of the fish, Jonah calms down and decides to stay alive. But when God causes the bush to wither and die, Jonah is furious all over again. What good is sitting in the chapel if you have to look out on a wicked city that isn't going up in smoke?

God has the last word in the story:

> You are concerned about the bush, for which you did not labor and which you did not grow; it came into being in a night and perished in a night. And should I not be concerned about Nineveh, that great city, in which there are more than a hundred and twenty thousand persons who do not know their right hand from their left, and also many animals? (4:10-11)

Jonah never answers God's question. That question is still hanging in the air today. How do we pray in the belly of the fish, in the innards of the sanctuary? Three years ago when we gathered in New York City to pray, "God bless America" came from a place of deep grief and fear. We sang in the light of votive candles in Union Square Park, surrounded by the flyers of the missing. *"Have you seen my father?"* We prayed for our beloved, broken city, our traumatized country. I don't know when the prayer turned, when the words began to sound different. The date is no more exact than the dating of the book of Jonah. We wrapped the prayer around us and shut out the rest of the world. "God bless America, land that I love." We didn't mention Nineveh.

Nineveh is the name of both an ancient city and a contemporary province in northern Iraq. The ruins of the Assyrian capital are now encompassed by the city of Mosul. A street in Bridgeport, Connecticut, has been renamed in memory of Tyanna Avery-Felder killed April seventh in Mosul. Attacks in Mosul averaged sixty per week in September.[16]

How do we pray in the sanctuary, in the belly of the Empire? Perhaps we no longer need to pray. In 2003 our country had a military presence in 153 of the 189 member countries of the United Nations.[17] Prayer shapes us even as we shape our prayers. Jonah might have been changed if he had prayed for Nineveh as

fervently as he prayed for himself. How shall we pray, you and I,
sitting here in this chapel in the belly of the Empire?

> God bless the world we love,
> Stranger and friend;
> Go before us, restore us
> With a hope that despair cannot end.
> Ev'ry people, ev'ry nation,
> Mighty ocean, heaven's dome.
> God bless the world we love,
> Our fragile home.
> God bless the world You love,
> Our fragile home.

Notes

Preface

1. Frederick Buechner, *Telling the Truth: The Gospel as Tragedy, Comedy & Fairy Tale* (San Francisco: Harper & Row, Publishers, 1977), 1.
2. Ibid., 13.
3. Ibid., 22.
4. Ibid., 23.
5. Ibid., 98.

1. Marking Time: Reading Scripture at the River's Edge

1. Chaim Stern, ed., *Gates of Repentance: The New Union Prayerbook for the Days of Awe* (New York: Central Conference of American Rabbis, 5738/1978), 293–94. Quotation used by permission.
2. Michael Fishbane, *The Exegetical Imagination: On Jewish Thought and Theology* (Cambridge, Mass.: Harvard University Press, 1998), 3.
3. Walter Brueggemann, *Texts That Linger, Words That Explode: Listening to Prophetic Voices* (Minneapolis: Fortress Press, 2000), 1.
4. "Confession of Faith," *Constitutions, Bylaws, and Continuing Resolutions of the Evangelical Lutheran Church in America*®, chapter 2.02.c (November 2005), 19.

5. Martin Luther, "Preface to the Epistles of St. James and St. Jude," in John Dillenberger, ed., *Martin Luther: Selections from His Writings* (Garden City, N.Y.: Anchor Books, 1961), 36:

> [James] does violence to Scripture, and so contradicts Paul and all Scripture. He tries to accomplish by emphasizing law what the apostles bring about by attracting men to love. I therefore refuse him a place among the writers of the true canon of my Bible . . .

6. David Carr, "Untamable Text of an Untamable God: Genesis and Rethinking the Character of Scripture," *Interpretation* 54, no. 4 (October 2000): 353:

> One might argue that such untamability is a problem, that we must find some way to stabilize interpretation so that it will yield a single meaning from the Bible. Yet I would argue the contrary. It is precisely the multi-voiced, untamable character of texts like Genesis that has served divergent faith communities through the ages.

7. Ibid., 353.

8. Walter Bruggemann, *Cadences of Home: Preaching among Exiles* (Louisville: Westminster John Knox Press, 1997), 76.

9. "Confession of Faith," *Constitutions, Bylaws, and Continuing Resolutions of the Evangelical Lutheran Church in America®*, chapter 2.03 (November 2005), 19.

10. Carr, 360.

11. Vincent L. Wimbush, "Reading Texts through Worlds, Worlds through Texts," in *Semeia* 62 (Atlanta: Scholars Press, 1993): 131.

12. Ibid., 137.

13. Ibid., 139.

14. Adele Berlin, "The Role of the Text in the Reading Process," in *Seimeia* 62 (Atlanta: Scholars Press, 1993): 143–44.

15. Ibid., 144–45.

16. Sandra M. Schneiders, *The Revelatory Text: Interpreting the New Testament as Sacred Scripture* (Collegeville, Minn.: The Liturgical Press, 1999), 61.

17. I am indebted to Victor Paul Furnish for this image of scripture as a family album, from an unpublished lecture at the Winter Pastors' School, Stetson University on January 27, 2004.

18. Schneiders, 61.

19. James R. Nieman, "An Ecclesiological Perspective on the Role of Scripture for Preaching," a paper presented at The Academy of Homiletics, December 2003, 64.

20. Ibid., 64–65.

21. I am grateful to Mary Boys for permission to use the following excerpt from her unpublished "(Christians) Interpreting Scripture: Some Guidelines."

> Imagine the two testaments as a conversational circle rather than in linear succession. At times this may mean using the Old (First) Testament for clarification; on other occasions, it may mean drawing upon its images or using it to bring out a particularly important dimension of God's self-revelation.

2. It Will Be All Right: New Rubrics for the Holy Man's Room

1. Walter Brueggemann, *Texts That Linger, Words That Explode: Listening to Prophetic Voices* (Minneapolis: Fortress Press, 2000), 1.

2. Terence E. Fretheim, *First and Second Kings (Westminster Bible Companion)* (Louisville: Westminster John Knox Press, 1999), 144.

3. Walter Brueggemann, *2 Kings (Knox Preaching Guides)* (Atlanta: Westminster John Knox Press, 1983), 17; Fretheim, 147.

4. D. Gerald Bostock, "Jesus as the New Elisha," *Expository Times* 92 (Edinburgh: T&T Clark Ltd.,1980): 40. See also Raymond E. Brown, "Jesus and Elisha," *Perspective* 12 (1971): 85–104.

5. A small sampling of feminist biblical texts written since 1976: Elisabeth Schüssler Fiorenza, *In Memory of Her: A Feminist Theological Reconstruction of Christian Origins* (Herder and Herder, 1983), and *Bread Not Stone: The Challenge of Feminist Biblical Interpretation* (Beacon Press, 1984); Adele Berlin, *Poetics and Interpretation of Biblical Narrative* (Sheffield Academic Press, 1983); Phyllis Trible, *God and the Rhetoric of Sexuality* (Fortress Press, 1978), *Texts of Terror: Literary-Feminist Readings of Biblical Narratives* (Fortress Press, 1984), and *Rhetorical Criticism: Context, Method, and the Book of Jonah* (Fortress Press, 1994); Letty Russell, ed., *Feminist Interpretation of the Bible* (Westminster John Knox, 1985); Adela Yarbro Collins, ed., *Feminist Perspectives on Biblical*

Scholarship (Society of Biblical Literature, 1985); J. Cheryl Exum, *Tragedy and Biblical Narrative: Arrows of the Almighty* (Cambridge University Press, 1992), *Fragmented Women: Feminist (Sub) versions of Biblical Narratives* (Trinity Press, 1993); J. Cheryl Exum and Johanna W. H. Bos, eds., *Semeia 42: Reasoning with the Foxes: Female Wit in a World of Male Power* (Society of Biblical Literature, 1988); Carol A. Newsom and Sharon H. Ringe, eds., *The Women's Bible Commentary* (Westminster John Knox, 1992); and too many others to list here.

6. Phyllis Trible, *God and the Rhetoric of Sexuality* (Philadelphia: Fortress Press, 1978), 202.

7. Fokkelien van Dijk-Hemmes, "The Great Woman of Shunem and the Man of God: A Dual Interpretation of 2 Kings 4.8-37," in Athalya Brenner, ed., *A Feminist Companion to the Bible* (Sheffield, England: Sheffield Academic Press, 1994), 219–30.

> Our story can, it seems, be interpreted as an extraordinary feast of patriarchal propaganda. According to patriarchal ideology, women have to become mothers whether they want to or not. (227)

Dijk-Hemmes doesn't stop with this negative patriarchal appraisal of the text but goes on to "wrestle a blessing" from the text, using the image of Jacob in Gen. 32:26. (See note 11 below.)

8. *Lutheran Book of Worship* (Minneapolis: Augsburg Publishing Company and Philadelphia: Board of Publication, Lutheran Church in America, 1978), 121.

9. Patrocinio Schweikart, "Reading Ourselves: Toward a Feminist Theory of Reading," in Elizabeth A. Flynn and Patrocinio P. Schweickart, eds., *Gender and Reading: Essays on Readers, Texts, and Contexts* (Baltimore and London: Johns Hopkins University Press, 1986), 42.

10. Larry Rasmussen, from an unpublished lecture.

11. Fokkelien van Dijk-Hemmes, 230:

> The memory of the "Great Woman" deserves to be kept alive. Moreover, the present woman (ly) reader can pay her the homage that the author and narrator of the biblical text withheld from her. The woman can be named. And what name is more appropriate than the adjective with which she is introduced? Her name is therefore here designated *Gedolah* . . . the "Great One."

12. Bruce M. Metzger and Roland E. Murphy, eds., *The New Oxford Annotated Bible with the Apocryphal/Deuterocanonical Books* (New York: Oxford University Press, 1991), 468.

13. Michael Fishbane, *The Exegetical Imagination: On Jewish Thought and Theology* (Cambridge, Mass.: Harvard University Press, 1998), 3.

14. L. DeAne Lagerquist, *From Our Mothers' Arms: A History of Women in the American Lutheran Church* (Minneapolis: Augsburg Publishing House, 1987).

> Diderikke Brandt, wife of a Luther College faculty member, organized women in Decorah, Iowa, in the 1860s to meet together and mend the clothing of the young pre-ministerial students (31).
>
> In 1919 the women instituted "Egg Sunday" to support the Church Extension Fund, which provided low-interest building loans to newly organized congregations. In rural areas women were asked to donate the value of the eggs they collected on Easter Sunday. Women without chickens were encouraged to find another means of contributing (57).
>
> Women's money allowed Lutheran congregations to make the transition from the tax-supported state churches of Europe to American denominations supported by voluntary contributions (41).

15. Martin Luther King Jr., *Why We Can't Wait* (New York: Harper & Row, 1963), 83. Copyright renewed 1991 Coretta Scott King. Reprinted by arrangement with the Heirs to the Estate of Martin Luther King Jr., c/o Writers House as agent for the proprietor, New York, N.Y.

16. Delores S. Williams, *Sisters in the Wilderness: The Challenge of Womanist God-Talk* (Maryknoll, N.Y.: Orbis Books, 1993). Williams lifts up the significance of the Hagar-Ishmael story in chapter 1, "Hagar's Story: A Route to Black Women's Issues":

> Hagar has "spoken" to generation after generation of black women because her story has been validated as true by suffering black people. She and Ishmael together, as family, model many black American families in which a lone woman/mother struggles to hold the family together in spite of the poverty to which ruling class economics consign it. Hagar, like many

black women, goes into the wide world to make a living for herself and her child, with only God by her side. (33)

17. Heidi Neumark, from an unpublished Bible study on 1 Kings 17 (the story of the prophet Elijah and the poor widow of Zarapheth); used by permission.

18. Barton Sutter, "The Snowman" from *The Book of Names: New and Selected Poems*. Copyright © 1993 by Barton Sutter. Reprinted with the permission of BOA Editions, Ltd., www.boaeditions.org.

19. Mordechai Cogan and Hayim Tadmor, *II Kings: Anchor Bible Commentary* (New York: Doubleday & Company, Inc., 1988), 57.

3. The Camel and the Cash Machine: A Story We Try to Forget

1. A sampling of those who hear flattery in the man's statement include: Kenneth E. Bailey, *Poet and Peasant and Through Peasant Eyes: A Literary-Cultural Approach to the Parable in Luke* (Grand Rapids: Eerdmans, 1980), 162; Vincent Taylor, *The Gospel According to St. Mark* (New York: St. Martin's Press, 1963), 425; Ched Myers, *Binding the Strong Man: A Political Reading of Mark's Story of Jesus* (Maryknoll, N.Y.: Orbis Books, 1988), 272.

Bonhoeffer also notes the man's self-centeredness in *The Cost of Discipleship* where he focuses on Matthew's version of this story (78–79).

2. Ched Myers says Jesus is intentional in adding, "Do not defraud," citing the work of Vincent Taylor:

In the Greek Bible the verb is appropriated to the act of *keeping back the wages* of a hireling, whereas in Classical Greek it is used of refusing to return goods or money deposited with another for safekeeping . . . (Taylor, 428)

3. Myers, 273.

4. W. H. Auden, "O Tell Me the Truth About Love," copyright 1940 & renewed 1968 by W. H. Auden, from *Collected Poems* by W. H. Auden. Used by permission of Random House, Inc. and Faber and Faber Ltd.

5. Alexis de Tocqueville cited by Leslie P. Norton, "The Wealth Revolution," *Barron's* 80, no. 38 (September 18, 2000): 33.

6. Patricia Leigh Brown, "Teaching Johnny Values Where Money Is King," *New York Times,* March 10, 2000, A14.

7. Leslie P. Norton, "The Wealth Revolution," 33.

8. James M. Childs, Jr., *Greed: Economics and Ethics in Conflict* (Minneapolis: Fortress Press, 2000), 36.

9. Graef S. Crystal, *In Search of Excess: The Overcompensation of American Executives* (New York and London: W. W. Norton & Company, 1991), 24–26.

10. Louis Uchitelle, "Working Families Strain to Live Middle-Class Life," *New York Times,* September 10, 2000, 28.

11. Holly Sklar, *Chaos or Community: Seeking Solutions, Not Scapegoats for Bad Economics* (Boston: South End Press, 1995), 14.

12. Sklar: "As a consequence of unconscionable poverty and government neglect, proportionately more children die before their first birthday in the United States than in 20 other countries. The death rate of Black babies in the US ranks 35th on the global scale, tied with Bulgaria and Chile, and behind such nations as Jamaica, Sri Lanka, Poland, Cuba and Kuwait" (15).

13. Ibid., 146.

14. Herman E. Daly and John B. Cobb, Jr., *For the Common Good: Redirecting the Economy toward Community, the Environment, and a Sustainable Future,* 2nd edition (Boston: Beacon Press, 1994). Daly and Cobb's work is summarized in Childs, 88:

> Increase in the GNP does not necessarily mean increase in economic welfare. That is, simple growth is not always simply good. It does not reveal how quality of life is faring under prevailing economic conditions. Instead, Daly and Cobb have developed a remarkable Index of Sustainable Economic Welfare, which records and correlates a number of factors, including equality of income distribution; improvement in health, education and public services; costs of pollution; loss of resources; and so on. (Daly and Cobb, 443ff)

15. Geoffrey Wheatcroft, "Politics Without Piety," *New York Times,* September 9, 2000, A27.

16. The long list of curses that will come upon those who do not obey the Lord God includes failures in every arena of life from land to cattle, fruit of the ground and of the womb. Plague and pestilence will overwhelm: "The LORD will strike you on the knees and on the legs

with grievous boils of which you cannot be healed, from the sole of your foot to the crown of your head" (Deuteronomy 28:35). Jesus describes Lazarus carefully: "And at his gate lay a poor man named Lazarus *covered with sores*, who longed to satisfy his hunger with what fell from the rich man's table; *even the dogs would come and lick his sores*" (Luke 16:20-21, italics mine). In Jesus' parable the poor man is not cursed but blessed, carried to Abraham's bosom.

17. Walter Brueggemann, *Deep Memory, Exuberant Hope: Contested Truth in a Post-Christian World* (Minneapolis: Fortress Press, 2000), 69.

18. Mary Ann Tolbert, *Sowing the Gospel: Mark's World in Literary-Historical Perspective* (Minneapolis: Fortress Press, 1996), 157.

19. Dietrich Bonhoeffer, *The Cost of Discipleship: Revised Edition* (New York: Macmillan Publishing Co., Inc., 1963), 76.

20. Ibid., 75–76.

21. Sharon Daloz Parks, "Household Economics," in Dorothy C. Bass, ed., *Practicing Our Faith: A Way of Life for Searching People* (San Francisco: Jossey-Bass, 1997), 46–47.

22. Ibid., 56.

23. Ibid., 56.

24. I am grateful to Pastor Joanne Engquist, co-pastor of University Lutheran Church in Cambridge, Massachusetts, for sharing this story and granting permission to use it.

4. Water on a Desert Road: Splashing in the Scroll of Isaiah

1. Cain Hope Felder, "Race, Racism, and the Biblical Narratives," in Cain Hope Felder, ed., *Stony the Road We Trod: African American Biblical Interpretation* (Minneapolis: Fortress Press, 1991), 141. See also Hans Conzelmann, *Acts of the Apostles: Hermeneia Series* (Philadelphia: Fortress Press, 1987), 68.

2. The adjectives quoted here are descriptions of African people used by Edward Long, a native Briton, in his history of Jamaica written in 1774. The text is cited by Larry E. Tise, *Proslavery: A History of the Defense of Slavery in America 1701–1840* (Athens, Ga: University of Georgia Press, 1987), 77–78.

3. Cottrel R. Carson, "'Do You Understand What You Are Reading?' A Reading of the Ethiopian Eunuch Story (Acts 8:26-40)

from a Site of Cultural Marronage" (PhD dissertation, New York: Union Theological Seminary, 1999), 156–60.

> An issue that must be addressed as part of a re-examination of verse 37's omission from the text of Acts is textual criticism's privileging of manuscripts whose production is attributed to the fourth and fifth centuries. Given the complex social and political dynamics that surrounded the church, Ethiopians, and eunuchs in the fourth and fifth centuries, our privileging of these manuscripts in a decision to omit verse 37 must be re-examined. (160)

4. Ephraim Syrus, *Hymn III* of "The Pearl, Seven Hymns on the Faith," trans. J. T. Sarsfield et al., in *Nicene and Post-Nicene Fathers of The Christian Church*, ed. Philip Schaff and Henry Wace, 2nd series, vol. 13, part 2 (Grand Rapids: Eerdmans, 1964), 295:

> The eunuch of Ethiopia upon his chariot saw Philip; the Lamb of Light met the dark man from out of the water. While he was reading, the Ethiopian was baptised and shone with joy, and journeyed on! . . .
> He made disciples and taught, and out of black men he made men white.

St. Jerome, "The Letters of St. Jerome: Letter 69, to Oceanus," trans. W. H. Fremantle et al., in *Nicene and Post-Nicene Fathers,* ed. P. Schaff and H. Wace, 2nd ser., vol. 6 (Grand Rapids: Eerdmans, 1957), 146:

> By reading of the prophet the eunuch of Candace the queen of Ethiopia is made ready for the baptism of Christ. Though it is against nature the Ethiopian does change his skin and the leopard his spots.

Cited by William P. Lawrence Jr., *The History of the Interpretation of Acts 8:26-40 by the Church Fathers Prior to the Fall of Rome* (PhD dissertation, New York City, Union Theological Seminary, 1984), 47 and 50; Ephraim Syrus (ca. 306–73) is also cited by Carson, 22–24; Jerome (ca. 347–420) is cited by Carson, 25–26.

5. Hans Conzelmann, *Acts of the Apostles: Hermeneia Series* (Philadelphia: Fortress Press, 1987), 68.

6. Carson, "Social Intertexture: Ancient Society's Knowledge of Eunuchs," 95–106, and "Cultural Intertexture: Eunuchs in LXX," 106–118.

7. Lewis A. Coser, *Greedy Institutions: Patterns of Undivided Commitment* (New York: Collier MacMillan), 23; cited by Carson, 96.

8. Carson, 98.

9. Ibid., 115–18.

10. Ibid., 102.

11. Ibid., 101–5. Carson cites the work of the following in describing the physical characteristics of eunuchs: Jacqueline Long, *Claudian's In Eutropium: Or How, When, and Why to Slander a Eunuch* (Chapel Hill: University of North Carolina Press, 1996), 108; John Bremer, *Asexualization* (New York: Macmillan, 1958), 82–83, 109–110; Ralph I. Dorfman and Reginald A. Shipley, *Androgens: Biochemistry, Physiology and Clinical Significance* (New York: Wiley, 1956) 208–9, 315–16.

12. Beverly Roberts Gaventa, "Ethiopian Eunuch," in David Noel Freedman, editor in chief, *Anchor Bible Dictionary*, vol. 2, D–G (New York: Doubleday, 1992), 667.

> Greek writers had long demonstrated a curiosity about and appreciation of Ethiopians as is evidenced in Homer's reference to Ethiopia as the "farthermost of men" (*Od.*,1.22–23) and in Herodotus' description of Ethiopians as the tallest and most handsome of all peoples (3.17–20). Luke's audience would have seen in the Ethiopian a positive figure, perhaps one to whom even an element of mystery would be attached because of his distant homeland.

See also Abraham Smith, "A Second Step in African Biblical Interpretation," in Fernando F. Segovia and Mary Ann Tolbert, eds., *Reading from this Place, Volume I: Social Location and Biblical Interpretation in the United States* (Minneapolis: Fortress Press, 1995), 227.

13. The Reform movement has adapted an older order of remembrance to include not only rabbis martyred in earlier centuries, but people of other nations and cultures:

> The earth's crust is soaked with the tears of the innocent. The blood of every race cries out from the ground. Which is the people without its martyrs?

Now, therefore, we honor those of every race and continent: the innocent, the victims, all our companions in death and our partners in grief. Them we honor, them we mourn: may they never be forgotten; may a better world grow out of their suffering. (Gates of Repentance, 430. Quotation used by permission.)

14. Gates of Repentance, 429–30. Quotation used by permission.

15. Robert Tannehill, The Narrative Unity of Luke-Acts: A Literary Interpretation: Volume 2: The Acts of the Apostles (Minneapolis: Fortress Press, 1994), 109; see also Luke Johnson, The Acts of the Apostles: Sacra Pagina Series, vol. 5 (Collegeville, Minn.: The Liturgical Press, 1992), 158; Carson, 119–24.

In Isaiah's vision, the household (oikos) of God includes eunuchs. The community envisioned by Isaiah is one in which only faithfulness to God defines inclusion . . .

What was a community expectation in Isaiah occurs in Acts. (Carson, 121, 122)

16. In addition to Cottrel R. Carson, a partial list of African-American biblical scholars who have brought new perspectives to the interpretation of Acts 8:26-40: Gay L. Byron, Symbolic Blackness and Ethnic Difference in Early Christian Literature (London and New York: Routledge, 2002); Cain Hope Felder, "Race, Racism and the Biblical Narratives," in Cain Hope Felder, ed., Stony the Road We Trod: African American Biblical Interpretation (Minneapolis: Fortress Press, 1991), 127–45; Clarice J. Martin, "The Function of Acts 8:26-40 within the Narrative Structure of the Book of Acts: The Significance of the Eunuch's Provenance for Acts 1:8c" (PhD dissertation, Duke University, 1996); Abraham Smith, "A Second Step in African American Biblical Interpretation: A Generic Reading Analysis of Acts 8:26-40," in Fernando E. Segovia and Mary Ann Tolbert, eds., Reading from this Place, Volume One: Social Location and Biblical Interpretation in the United States (Minneapolis: Fortress Press, 1995), 213–28; Prince Vuyani Ntintili, "The Presence and Role of Africans in the Bible," The Holy Bible: African American Jubilee Edition (New York: American Bible Society, 1995), 95–107.

17. Bradley S. Artson, "Gay and Lesbian Jews: An Innovative Jewish Legal Position," Jewish Spectator (Winter, 1990): 12. Artson's article reviews only Jewish texts, but similar arguments have been raised by

New Testament scholars citing the reality that the term *homosexuality* was unknown by biblical writers:

> Homosexuality as an orientation (as opposed to oppressive or anonymous same-sex acts) is not mentioned in the Torah or halakhah, let alone prohibited. We are dealing not with previously considered and previously outlawed phenomena, but with a situation never before encountered in Jewish law. Modern homosexual love and stable homosexual couples are different in significant respects from anything known in the Torah or in rabbinic Judaism (Artson, 12).

Krister Stendahl reminds us that the term "homosexual" is quite recent: "German psychologists in the 1890s seem to have invented the term, and it soon came into English, although it did not make the Oxford English Dictionary until its Supplement in the 1930s." "Can Bishops Tell the Truth as They See It?" in Deborah A. Brown, ed., *Christianity in the 21st Century* (New York: Crossroad Publishing, 2000), 188.

18. Michael Fishbane, *The Exegetical Imagination: On Jewish Thought and Theology* (Cambridge: Harvard University Press, 1998), 3.

19. Carson, 105:

> Pre-puberal eunuchs were perpetual outsiders in Greco-Roman society. Their social functions, particularly in the domestic arena, and their appearance caused members of the dominant culture to view them as outside the *oikos*—if not physically, certainly emotionally.

20. Jacqueline Long, *Claudian's In Eutropium*, 124–25.

21. Audre Lorde, *A Burst of Light* (Ithaca: Firebrand Books, 1988), 120.

22. Merlyn E. Satrom in "A Collection of Responses from ELCA Academicians and Synodical Bishops to *The Church and Human Sexuality: A Lutheran Perspective*" (Chicago: Division for Church in Society, Evangelical Lutheran Church in America, 1994), 186:

> From the New Testament, I Corinthians 6:9f and I Timothy 1:8ff use the Greek words *malakoi* and *arsenokoitai*, which most agree are difficult to define. Even though lexicographers agree

that some form of homosexual activity is referred to with these words, there is no certainty about their meaning . . .

23. For a thorough and thought-provoking discussion of the relationship between church teaching on divorce and remarriage, and church teaching on gay and lesbian unions see Mary Ann Tolbert, "Expert Testimony on Holy Unions for the Committee on Investigation"; Northern California-Nevada Annual Conference of The United Methodist Church (February 2000), accessed via http://www.psr.edu/page.cfm?l=62&id=106.

24. Though there are many examples of selective literalism (e.g., holiness codes discarded), I will note only the following text describing the practices of early Christian communities:

> Now the whole group of those who believed were of one heart and soul, and no one claimed private ownership of any possessions, but everything they owned was held in common. With great power the apostles gave their testimony to the resurrection of the Lord Jesus, and great grace came upon them all. There was not a needy person among them, for as many as owned lands or houses sold them and brought the proceeds to the apostles' feet, and it was distributed to each as any had need. (Acts 4:32-34)

Few would argue that individual church members, congregations, or denominations take this text (or a similar passage in Acts 2:44-47) literally.

25. Stendahl, 188.

26. Rabbi Yaakov Levado (a pseudonym), "Gayness and God: Wrestlings of an Orthodox Rabbi," *Tikkun*, 8:5, 58, 59.

27. I am grateful to Dr. Edwina Wright, Assistant Professor of Old Testament at Union Theological Seminary, for her insights into the Hebrew *yad vashem*, and to Rabbi Margaret Moers Wenig for connecting Isaiah's term with the holocaust memorial in Jerusalem.

28. Levado, 59.

29. Stendahl, 188. Earlier in this chapter, Stendahl wrote:

> To cut a long story short, I think the two foci of a Christian teaching on responsible sexuality are *fidelity* and *mutuality*. While the church traditionally has been forceful in teaching

fidelity, the church's record on mutuality has been weak, indeed . . .

As the churches assess their teaching about sexuality, it would be reasonable to expect that Item One on the agenda should be a radical repentance for the dehumanizing neglect of mutuality as one of the two cornerstones of our sexuality, a cornerstone that became a stumbling block. (187)

30. Tannehill, 110:

The two scenes of the Ethiopian eunuch and Cornelius are related to each other according to a pattern established in the Samaritan mission and later repeated in Antioch ([Acts] 11:19-24): the new step is taken by someone other than the apostles, and the apostles must then catch up with events that are happening independently of them. In the process the rightness of the new move is verified.

31. Robert Lowry, "Shall We Gather at the River." This hymn was the processional hymn for the beginning of the Beecher Lecture series in October 2000. Everyone was invited to join in the chorus at the close of this last lecture.

5. Standing Once More at the River's Edge

1. Eva Jensen, "Lutheran Liberian Women Unify for Peace," *Lutheran Woman Today* (January/February 2004): 2; used by permission.
2. Ibid., 2.
3. Liberia Support Network: http://www.elca.org/liberia/news/gbowee-gme2004.html.
4. Cited in Thomas Frank, *What's the Matter with Kansas? How Conservatives Won the Heart of America* (New York: Henry Holt and Company, 2004), n. 2, 266–67.
5. Ibid., 205.
6. Ibid., 6.
7. Ibid., 127.
8. Garrison Keillor, *Homegrown Democrat: A Few Plain Thoughts from the Heart of America* (New York: Viking Press, 2004), 194.

9. Cited by Stephen Chapman in Wes Avram, ed., *Anxious about Empire: Theological Essays on the New Global Realities* (Grand Rapids: Brazos Press, 2004), 91.

10. Doug Pritchard, "Tom's Last Journey," CPT news release quoted in *SoJo Mail*, March 13, 2006.

11. "We Mourn the Loss of Tom Fox," CPT Release: http://www.cpt.org/iraq/response/06-10-03statement.htm.

12. Heidi Neumark, "Beautiful Feet," in David Polk, ed., *Shaken Foundations: Sermons from America's Pulpits after the Terrorist Attacks* (St. Louis: Chalice Press, 2001), 28.

13. Neumark, 33.

6. Sermons Preached at the River's Edge

1. Dietrich Bonhoeffer, *Letters and Papers from Prison*, ed. Eberhard Bethge, enlarged ed. (New York: Macmillan, 1971), 219.

2. Ibid., 220.

3. Ibid., 220.

4. Alan Greenspan quoted in Bill Goldstein, "Word for Word / 'Greenspan Shrugged'; When Greed Was Virtue and Regulation the Enemy," *New York Times*, July 21, 2002.

5. "The Network for Inclusive Vision" is a group of clergy and laypeople within the Evangelical Lutheran Church in America advocating the ordination of non-celibate gay and lesbian people. "Word Alone" came into being to oppose full communion between the ELCA and the Episcopal Church/USA primarily over the issue of apostolic succession. More recently, many members of "Word Alone" have also registered their opposition to blessing same-gender relationships and the ordination of gay men and lesbians.

6. Krister Stendahl, "What Does It Mean to Be a Reforming Church?" in Charles Lutz, ed., *A Reforming Church . . . Gift and Task: Essays from a Free Conference* (Minneapolis: Kirk House Publishers, 1995), 32.

7. Bishop Peter Rogness, "Letter to the St. Paul Area Synod," January 2003; used by permission.

8. Romans 1:26-27 is often cited as the most important text in debates about homosexuality: "For this reason God gave them up to degrading passions. Their women exchanged natural intercourse for

unnatural, and in the same way also the men, giving up natural inter-course with women, were consumed with passion for one another. Men committed shameless acts with men and received in their own persons the due penalty for their error." Though this text seems definitive for many, there are widely divergent views on what Paul actually means. For example, "women exchanged natural intercourse for unnatural" could have meant anything other than a male-dominant position in sexual intercourse.

9. "Vision and Expectations" is a document published by the Evangelical Lutheran Church in America outlining guidelines for ordi-nation of pastors and Associates in Ministry.

10. "The Defense Monitor," November/December 2003, vol. 32:5 (Washington: Center for Defense Information, 2003): 5.

11. Chalmers Johnson, *The Sorrows of Empire: Militarism, Secrecy, and the End of the Republic* (New York: Henry Holt and Company, 2004), 4.

12. "Keeping Earth Fit for Development," *New York Times,* September 6, 2002, A22.

13. Http://www.globalsecurity.org/military/world/iraq/mosul.htm (October 10, 2004), 3.

14. Phyllis Trible, *Rhetorical Criticism: Context, Method, and the Book of Jonah* (Minneapolis: Fortress Press, 1994), 172.

15. Http://www.globalsecurity.org/military/world/iraq/mosul.htm (October 10, 2004), 3–4.

16. "Bridgeport street renamed Tyanna Avery-Felder Boulevard": many sources including www.newsday.com. Statistics about attacks in Mosul from Associated Press article by Jim Krane, "Iraq violence eclipses rosy declarations": several sites including www.bismarcktribune (September 24, 2004).

17. Johnson, *The Sorrows of Empire*, 288.